FROM BED TO VERSE

FROM BED TO VERSE

An Unashamed Pillow Book

compiled by

MARTIN SEYMOUR-SMITH

SOUVENIR PRESS

ISBN 0 285 63050 4

Photoset and printed in Great Britain by
Redwood Press Limited, Melksham, Wiltshire

This anthology is dedicated to Michael Thorne

Contents

Contents

THE ONE AND ONLY

Contents

Contents

OUTRAGE AND REMORSE

BANDIED WOMEN

Contents

PLIGHT

SATIRICAL

WHORING

DISGUST

Contents

Introduction

This is an anthology of explicit English poetry about lust, whether accompanied by feelings of love or (as we see in so many examples here) not. It is not quite an anthology of 'erotic verse', for it seems to me that, despite a recent definition of this as dealing 'with the sexual in more or less explicit detail', erotic verse has very often been forced to be quite deliberately non-explicit. Some Victorian poets of note failed even to be aware of the fact that they were expressing their erotic feelings (a polite name for lusts), and so 'Freudian' analyses of such poetry (by, for example, Browning as well as by his wife) have become two-a-penny and sometimes tiresome. Even Thomas Hardy, who was well aware of the carnal nature of his feelings, was unable to be explicit, and so cannot qualify for inclusion here. The poems in this collection, by contrast, even when they do not go very far into exploration of the physical, are never reticent. They are not inhibited. But, given that, they do vary: from the charmingly delicate intimations of William Strode's 'On Westwell Downs', or the complex hints of Empson's 'Aubade', to the savagely obscene, direct and provocative, such as Wilkes' two outrageous poems parodying well-known hymns.

So nineteenth-century poetry is almost entirely excluded from *From Bed to Verse*, simply on the grounds that it is not an anthology of oblique but of direct eroticism. It is true that physical sexual feelings have never been easy to ignore, as the Victorians discovered by their experiment of avoiding candour about them. It is true, also, that the Victorian habit was to erect (and I use the word advisedly) such strict prohibitions around the subject of sex, that these were titillating in themselves . . . They even invented such 'diseases' as 'spermatorrhea' (just the stickiness that is the result of unfulfilled erections) . . . But to compile an anthology of Victorian poems that were almost comically erotic just when they meant not to be would have been quite a different exercise, and it is not what I wanted to do here. An alternative would have been to print deliberately obscene verse of the Victorian period — but none of this is very good. It was no more than unusual in the polite context of its time, and it now reads no more than amusingly at its very best. The poems by Wilkes here — pre-Victorian, of course, but written at a time when Victorian prohibitions were coming into being — come nearest to the novel and merely amusing; but I have included them because they are seldom reprinted, because they are of historical importance, and because they are quite clever in the way in which they imitate their originals. They succeeded in their purpose of causing the maximum possible offence.

I should have liked to include Chaucer, but his language is not quite comprehensible to the general reader who has not studied Middle English, and he does not translate well. I have not in fact included any poem that is not easily understandable; but I have added a few glosses.

Like everyone else, I have been much amused by Gavin Ewart's light verse, from *Phallus in Wonderland* (which he wrote, I believe, at the age of seventeen) onwards; but I have felt that it, and its like (by A. P. Herbert and many others), was a trifle inconsequential for this kind of anthology, which, although it is not always serious (God forbid), verges on the serious in that it tries to represent English poets being candid about their needs, enjoyments, regrets and disgusts. This is not to say that there is not a fair sprinkling of popular, decent verse in celebration of sexual activity. But to be simply smutty has not been enough. However, poems (such as Marvell's 'To His Coy Mistress') have not been excluded by reason of their fame, so long as that fame is deserved. They belong here, and so they are here. They can bear re-reading, too: we may all suffer from knowing them less well than we think we do.

There was not much prudery in English verse before the advent of puritanism in the reign of Elizabeth I. The puritans could not prevent poets like Robert Herrick writing as they did; but the Restoration reaction to their rule is well known. It is fully represented here, mainly in the desperate and disgusted poems of John Wilmot, Earl of Rochester, an important influence in English poetry and a great poet in his own right. The vein initiated by him (and, to a lesser extent, his friends such as Etherege) continued through Swift, who added his own brand of disgust, culminated in Wilkes' deliberately outrageous, and not really at all poetic *Essay on Women* (not included here), became submerged by gentility, but then re-emerged in Graves, whose debt to Rochester is obvious.

But my presentation ignores chronology, just as it ignores taking sides in any debate there may be about the desirability of continuing sexual activity between men and women (I am thinking of some radical lesbians). The book is divided into unequal sections: *Desire, Persuasion, Enjoyment, The One and Only* (in praise of women by men, as it turns out — there is not too much in English verse by women praising men: they either praise each other or, very understandably, attack men), *Counsel* (a catch-all for all kinds of opinions that do not quite qualify as persuasive), *Marriage, Dreams, Dilemmas* (which, I should hasten to add, are almost all, being by males, attributive — readers are encouraged to disagree as vigorously as possible), *Outrage and Remorse, Bandied Women, Plight, Satirical, Whoring, Disgust,* and *Impotence and Abstention*. There are other categories in which poems about so universal a practice as lovemaking (or wanting to lovemake) could be divided; but not many better, I think, or very different.

Finally: the publishers and I decided to exclude homosexual poems only because we thought that these might better form the subject of a separate anthology. We have also excluded poetry in languages other than English, mainly because of the lack of suitable translations. But I wish I could have included some of the poems of the twentieth-century Japanese poet Hagiwara, which would have interested even those readers who did not subsequently follow his advice (I cannot comment on its effectiveness, either, never having tried it): he recommended that sex for men take place 'under the watchful eye of the bridegroom's mother'. Alas, he, too, is untranslatable.

I am deeply grateful to Richard Acam for helping with this anthology in ways too numerous to mention here.

Martin Seymour-Smith,
Brownbread Street
April 1991

DESIRE

Virgin Youth

Now and again
The life that looks through my eyes
And quivers in words through my mouth,
And behaves like the rest of men,
Slips away, so I gasp in surprise.
And then
My unknown breasts begin
To wake, and down the thin
Ripples below the breast an urgent
Rhythm starts, and my silent and slumberous belly
In one moment rouses insurgent.

My soft, slumbering belly,
Quivering awake with one impulse and one will,
Then willy nilly
A lower me gets up and greets me;
Homunculus stirs from his roots, and strives until,
Risen up, he beats me.

He stands, and I tremble before him.
— Who then art thou? —
He is wordless, but sultry and vast,
And I can't deplore him.
— Who art thou? What hast
Thou to do with me, thou lustrous one, iconoclast? —

How beautiful he is! without sound,
Without eyes, without hands;
Yet, flame of the living ground
He stands, the column of fire by night.
And he knows from the depths; he quite
Alone understands.

Quite alone, he alone
Understands and knows.
Lustrously sure, unknown
Out of nowhere he rose.

I tremble in his shadow, as he burns
For the dark goal.
He stands like a lighthouse, night churns
Round his base, his dark light rolls
Into darkness, and darkly returns.

Is he calling, the lone one? Is his deep
Silence full of summons?
Is he moving invisibly? Does his steep
Curve sweep towards a woman's?

Traveller, column of fire,
It is vain.
The glow of thy full desire
Becomes pain.

Dark, ruddy pillar, forgive me! I
Am helplessly bound
To the rock of virginity. Thy
Strange voice has no sound.

We cry in the wilderness. Forgive me, I
Would so gladly lie
In the womanly valley, and ply
Thy twofold dance.

Thou dark one, thou proud, curved beauty! I
Would worship thee, letting my buttocks prance.
But the hosts of men with one voice deny
Me the chance.

They have taken the gates from the hinges
And built up the way. I salute thee
But to deflower thee. Thy tower impinges
On nothingness. Pardon me!

D. H. LAWRENCE

From Pent-up Aching Rivers

From pent-up aching rivers,
From that of myself without which I were nothing,
From what I am determin'd to make illustrious, even if
    I stand sole among men,
From my own voice resonant, singing the phallus,
Singing the song of procreation,
Singing the need of superb children and therein superb
    grown people,
Singing the muscular urge and the blending,
Singing the bedfellow's song, (O resistless yearning!
O for any and each the body correlative attracting!
O for you whoever you are your correlative body! O it,
    more than all else, you delighting!)
From the hungry gnaw that eats me night and day,
From native moments, from bashful pains, singing
    them,
Seeking something yet unfound though I have
    diligently sought it many a long year,
Singing the true song of the soul fitful at random,
Renascent with grossest Nature or among animals,
Of that, of them and what goes with them my poems
    informing,
Of the smell of apples and lemons, of the pairing of
    birds,
Of the wet of woods, of the lapping of waves,
Of the mad pushes of waves upon the land, I them
    chanting,
The overture lightly sounding, the strain anticipating,
The welcome nearness, the sight of the perfect body,
The swimmer swimming naked in the bath, or
    motionless on his back lying and floating,
The female form approaching, I pensive, love-flesh
    tremulous aching,
The divine list for myself or you or for any one making,

The face, the limbs, the index from head to foot, and
    what it arouses,
The mystic deliria, the madness amorous, the utter
    abandonment,
(Hark close and still what I now whisper to you,
I love you, O you entirely possess me,
O that you and I escape from the rest and go utterly
    off, free and lawless,
Two hawks in the air, two fishes swimming in the sea
    not more lawless than we;)
The furious storm through me careering, I passionately
    trembling,
The oath of the inseparableness of two together, of the
    woman that loves me and whom I love more than
    my life, that oath swearing,
(O I willingly stake all for you,
O let me be lost if it must be so!
O you and I! what is it to us what the rest do or think?
What is all else to us? only that we enjoy each other
    and exhaust each other if it must be so;)
From the master, the pilot I yield the vessel to,
The general commanding me, commanding all, from
    him permission taking,
From time the programme hastening, (I have loiter'd
    too long as it is,)
From sex, from the warp and from the woof,
From privacy, from frequent repinings alone,
From plenty of persons near and yet the right person
    not near,
From the soft sliding of hands over me and thrusting of
    fingers through my hair and beard,
From the long sustain'd kiss upon the mouth or
    bosom,

Desire

From the close pressure that makes me or any man
    drunk, fainting with excess,
From what the divine husband knows, from the work
    of fatherhood,
From exultation, victory and relief, from the
    bedfellow's embrace in the night,
From the act-poems of eyes, hands, hips and bosoms,
From the cling of the trembling arm,
From the bending curve and the clinch,
From side by side to pliant coverlet off-throwing,
From the one so unwilling to have me leave, and me
    just as unwilling to leave,
(Yet a moment O tender waiter, and I return,)
From the hour of shining stars and dropping dews,
From the night a moment I emerging flitting out,
Celebrate you act divine and you children prepared for,
And you stalwart loins.

WALT WHITMAN
from _Children of Adam_

A Woman Waits for Me

A woman waits for me, she contains all, nothing is
    lacking,
Yet all were lacking if sex were lacking, or if the moisture
    of the right man were lacking.

Sex contains all, bodies, souls,
Meanings, proofs, purities, delicacies, results,
    promulgations,
Songs, commands, health, pride, the maternal mystery,
    the seminal milk,
All hopes, benefactions, bestowals, all the passions,
    loves, beauties, delights of the earth,
All the governments, judges, gods, follow'd persons of
    the earth,
These are contain'd in sex as parts of itself and
    justifications of itself.

Without shame the man I like knows and avows the
    deliciousness of his sex,
Without shame the woman I like knows and avows hers.

Now I will dismiss myself from impassive women,
I will go stay with her who waits for me, and with those
    women that are warm-blooded and sufficient for me,
I see that they understand me and do not deny me,
I see that they are worthy of me, I will be the robust
    husband of those women.

They are not one jot less than I am,
They are tann'd in the face by shining suns and blowing
    winds,
Their flesh has the old divine suppleness and strength,
They know how to swim, row, ride, wrestle, shoot, run,
    strike, retreat, advance, resist, defend themselves,

They are ultimate in their own right — they are calm,
    clear, well-possess'd of themselves.

I draw you close to me, you women,
I cannot let you go, I would do you good,
I am for you, and you are for me, not only for our own
    sake, but for others' sakes,
Envelop'd in you sleep greater heroes and bards,
They refuse to awake at the touch of any man but me.

It is I, you women, I make my way,
I am stern, acrid, large, undissuadable, but I love you,
I do not hurt you any more than is necessary for you,
I pour the stuff to start sons and daughters fit for these
    States, I press with slow rude muscle,
I brace myself effectually, I listen to no entreaties,
I dare not withdraw till I deposit what has so long
    accumulated within me.

Through you I drain the pent-up rivers of myself,
In you I wrap a thousand onward years,
On you I graft the grafts of the best-beloved of me and
    America,
The drops I distil upon you shall grow fierce and athletic
    girls, new artists, musicians, and singers,
The babes I beget upon you are to beget babes in their
    turn,
I shall demand perfect men and women out of my love-
    spendings,
I shall expect them to interpenetrate with others, as I and
    you interpenetrate now,
I shall count on the fruits of the gushing showers of
    them, as I count on the fruits of the gushing showers
    I give now,

I shall look for loving crops from the birth, life, death,
immortality, I plant so lovingly now.

WALT WHITMAN
from *Children of Adam*

Let not us

Let not us that young men be
From Venus' ways banished be.
Though that age with great disdain
Would have youth from love refrain,
In their minds consider you must
How they did in their most lust.

For if they were in like case,
And would then have gotten grace,
They may not now then gainsay
That which then was most their joy.
Wherefore indeed the truth to say,
It is for youth the meetest play.

ANON

On Westwell Downs

When Westwell Downs I 'gan to tread,
Where cleanly winds the green did sweep,
Methought a landscape there was spread,
Here a bush and there a sheep;
    The pleated wrinkles on the face
    Of wave-swoln earth did lend such grace,
    As shadowings in imagery
    Which both deceive and please the eye.

The sheep sometimes did tread a maze
By often winding in and in,
And sometimes round about they trace
Which milkmaids call a fairy ring.
    Such semi-circles have they run,
    Such lines across so trimly spun,
    That shepherds learn, whene'er they please,
    A new geometry with ease.

Here and there two hilly crests
Amidst them hug a pleasant green,
And these are like two swelling breasts
That close a tender fall between.
    Here could I read or sleep or pray
    From early morn till flight of day:
    But hark! a sheep's bell calls me up,
    Like Oxford college bells, to sup.

WILLIAM STRODE

Desire

A Prayer to the Wind

Go, thou gentle whispering wind,
Bear this sigh, and if thou find
Where my cruel fair doth rest
Cast it in her snowy breast,
So, inflamed by my desire,
It may set her heart afire.
Those sweet kisses thou shalt gain,
Will reward thee for thy pain;
Boldly light upon her lip,
There suck odours, and thence skip
To her bosom; lastly fall
Down, and wander over all.
Range about those ivory hills,
From whose every part distils
Amber dew; there spices grow,
There pure streams of nectar flow;
There perfume thyself, and bring
All those sweets upon thy wing.
As thou return'st, change by thy power
Every weed into a flower;
Turn each thistle to a vine,
Make the bramble eglantine;
For so rich a booty made,
Do but this, and I am paid.
Thou can'st with thy powerful blast
Heat apace, and cool as fast;
Thou can'st kindle hidden flame,
And again destroy the same:
Then, for pity, either stir
Up the fire of love in her,
That alike both flames may shine,
Or else quite extinguish mine.

THOMAS CAREW

Nothing to Fear

All fixed: early arrival at the flat
Lent by a friend, whose note says *Lucky sod*;
Drinks on the tray; the cover-story pat
And quite uncheckable; her husband off
Somewhere with all the kids till six o'clock
(Which ought to be quite long enough):
And all worth while: face really beautiful,
Good legs and hips, and as for breasts — my God.
What about guilt, compunction and such stuff?
I've had my fill of all that cock;
It'll wear off, as usual.

Yes, all fixed. Then why this slight trembling,
Dry mouth, quick pulse-rate, sweaty hands,
As though she were the first? No, not impatience,
Nor fear of failure, thank you, Jack.
Beauty, they tell me, is a dangerous thing,
Whose touch will burn, but I'm asbestos, see?
All worth while — it's a dead coincidence
That sitting here, a bag of glands
Tuned up to concert pitch, I seem to sense
A different style of caller at my back,
As cold as ice, but just as set on me.

KINGSLEY AMIS

14

PERSUASION

To His Coy Mistress

Had we but world enough, and time,
This coyness, lady, were no crime.
We would sit down, and think which way
To walk, and pass our long love's day.
Thou by the Indian Ganges' side
Shouldst rubies find: I by the tide
Of Humber would complain. I would
Love you ten years before the flood,
And you should, if you please, refuse
Till the conversion of the Jews;
My vegetable love should grow
Vaster than empires and more slow;
An hundred years should go to praise
Thine eyes, and on thy forehead gaze;
Two hundred to adore each breast,
But thirty thousand to the rest;
An age at least to every part,
And the last age should show your heart.
For, lady, you deserve this state,
Nor would I love at lower rate.
  But at my back I always hear
Time's wingèd chariot hurrying near,
And yonder all before us lie
Deserts of vast eternity.
Thy beauty shall no more be found,
Nor, in thy marble vault shall sound
My echoing song; then worms shall try
That long-preserved virginity,
And your quaint honour turn to dust,
And into ashes all my lust:
The graves a fine and private place,
But none I think do there embrace.
  Now therefore, while the youthful hue
Sits on thy skin like morning dew,
And while thy willing soul transpires

At every pore with instant fires,
Now let us sport us while we may,
And now, like amorous birds of prey,
Rather at once our time devour,
That languish in this slow-chapt power.
Let us roll all our strength and all
Our sweetness up into one ball,
And tear our pleasures with rough strife,
Through the iron gates of life;
Thus, though we cannot make our sun
Stand still, yet we will make him run.

ANDREW MARVELL

The Resolute Courtier

Prithee, say aye or no;
If thou 'lt not have me, tell me so;
     I cannot stay,
     Nor will I wait upon
     A smile or frown.
If thou wilt have me, say;
Then I am thine, or else I am mine own.

Be white or black; I hate
Dependence on a checkered fate;
     Let go, or hold;
     Come, either kiss or not:
     Now to be hot,
     And then again as cold,
Is a fantastic fever you have got.

A tedious woo is base,
And worse by far than a long grace:
     For whilst we stay,
     Our lingering spoils the roast,
     Or stomach's lost;
     Nor can, nor will I stay;
For if I sup not quickly, I will fast.

Whilst we are fresh and stout
And vigorous, let us to 't:
     Alas, what good
     From wrinkled man appears,
     Gelded with years,
     When his thin wheyish blood
Is far less comfortable than his tears?

THOMAS SHIPMAN

Upon a Favour Offered

Celia, too late you would repent:
　The offering all your store
Is now but like a pardon sent
　To one that 's dead before.

While at the first you cruel proved,
　And grant the bliss too late;
You hindered me of one I loved,
　To give me one I hate.

I thought you innocent as fair
　When first my court I made;
But when your falsehoods plain appear,
　My love no longer stayed.

Your bounty of those favours shown,
　Whose worth you first deface,
Is melting valued medals down
　And giving us the brass.

Oh, since the thing we beg 's a toy
　That 's prized by love alone,
Why cannot women grant the joy
　Before our love is gone?

WILLIAM WALSH

Love's Courtship

Kiss, lovely Celia, and be kind;
Let my desires freedom find,
    Sit thee down,
And we will make the gods confess
Mortals enjoy some happiness.

Mars would disdain his mistress' charms
If he beheld thee in my arms,
    And descend,
Thee his mortal queen to make,
Or live as mortal for thy sake.

Venus must lose her title now,
And leave to brag of Cupid's bow;
    Silly Queen!
She hath but one, but I can spy
Ten thousand Cupids in thy eye.

Nor may the sun behold our bliss,
For sure thy eyes do dazzle his;
    If thou fear
That he'll betray thee with his light,
Let me eclipse thee from his sight!

And while I shade thee from his eye
Oh! let me hear thee gently cry,
    Celia yields!
Maids often lose their maidenhead,
Ere they set foot in nuptial bed.

THOMAS CAREW

To His Mistress Going to Bed

Come, Madam, come, all rest my powers defy,
Until I labour, I in labour lie.
The foe oft-times having the foe in sight,
Is tired with standing though they never fight.
Off with that girdle, like heaven's zone glistering,
But a far fairer world encompassing.
Unpin that spangled breastplate which you wear,
That th' eyes of busy fools may be stopped there.
Unlace yourself, for that harmonious chime
Tells me from you, that now 'tis your bed time.
Off with that happy busk, which I envy,
That still can be, and still can stand so nigh.
Your gown going off, such beauteous state reveals,
As when from flowery meads th' hill's shadow steals.
Off with that wiry coronet and show
The hairy diadem which on you doth grow;
Now off with those shoes, and then safely tread
In this love's hallowed temple, this soft bed.
In such white robes heaven's angels used to be
Received by men; thou angel bring'st with thee
A heaven like Mahomet's paradise; and though
Ill spirits walk in white, we easily know
By this these angels from an evil sprite,
Those set our hairs, but these our flesh upright.
    Licence my roving hands, and let them go
Before, behind, between, above, below.
O my America, my new found land,
My kingdom, safeliest when with one man manned,
My mine of precious stones, my empery,
How blessed am I in this discovering thee!
To enter in these bonds, is to be free;
Then where my hand is set, my seal shall be.
    Full nakedness, all joys are due to thee.
As souls unbodied, bodies unclothed must be,
To taste whole joys. Gems which you women use

Are like Atlanta's balls, cast in men's views,
That when a fool's eye lighteth on a gem,
His earthly soul may covet theirs, not them.
Like pictures, or like books' gay coverings made
For laymen, are all women thus arrayed;
Themselves are mystic books, which only we
Whom their imputed grace will dignify
Must see revealed. Then since I may know,
As liberally, as to a midwife, show
Thyself: cast all, yea, this white linen hence,
Here is no penance, much less innocence.
  To teach thee, I am naked first, why then
What needst thou have more covering than a man.

JOHN DONNE

ENJOYMENT

from *Homage to Sextus Propertius*

Me happy, night, night full of brightness;
Oh couch made happy by my long delectations;
How many words talked out with abundant candles;
Struggles when the lights were taken away;
Now with bared breasts she wrestled against me,
    Tunic spread in delay;
And she then opening my eyelids fallen in sleep,
Her lips upon them; and it was her mouth saying:
    Sluggard!

In how many varied embraces, our changing arms,
Her kisses, how many, lingering on my lips.
'Turn not Venus into a blinded motion,
    Eyes are the guides of love,
Paris took Helen naked coming from the bed of
    Menelaus,
Endymion's naked body, bright bait for Diana,'
    — such at least is the story.

While our fates twine together, sate we our eyes with
    love;
For long night comes upon you
               and a day when no day returns.
Let the gods lay chains upon us
          so that no day shall unbind them.

Fool who would set a term to love's madness,
For the sun shall drive with black horses,
    earth shall bring wheat from barley,
The flood shall move toward the fountain
    Ere love know moderations,
    The fish shall swim in dry streams.
No, now while it may be, let not the fruit of life cease.

    Dry wreaths drop their petals,
        their stalks are woven in baskets,

To-day we take the great breath of lovers,
  to-morrow fate shuts us in.

Though you give all your kisses
                    you give but few.

Nor can I shift my pains to other,
    Hers will I be dead,
If she confer such nights upon me,
                long is my life, long in years,
If she give me many,
        God am I for the time.

                              EZRA POUND

Women

Give me a Girl (if one I needs must meet)
Or in her Nuptial, or her winding sheet;
I know but two good Hours that women have,
One in the Bed, another in the Grave.
Thus of the whole Sex all I would desire,
Is to enjoy their Ashes, or their Fire.

WILLIAM CARTWRIGHT

Who shall have my fair lady?

Who shall have my fair lady?
 Who shall have my fair lady?
Who but I, who but I, who but I?
 Under the leavès green!

The fairest man
That best love can,
Dandirly, dandirly, dandirly dan,
 Under the leavès green!

ANON

Sylvia the fair

Sylvia, the fair, in the bloom of fifteen,
Felt an innocent warmth as she lay on the green;
She had heard of a pleasure, and something she guessed
By the towzing, and tumbling, and touching her breast.
She saw the men eager, but was at a loss,
What they meant by their sighing, and kissing so close;
    By their praying and whining
    And clasping and twining,
    And panting and wishing,
    And sighing and kissing,
  And sighing and kissing so close.

'Ah!' she cried, 'ah! for a languishing maid,
In a country of Christians, to die without aid!
Not a Whig, or a Tory, or Trimmer at least,
Or a Protestant parson, or Catholic priest,
To instruct a young virgin, that is at a loss,
What they meant by their sighing and kissing so close!
    By their praying and whining,
    And clasping and twining,
    And panting and wishing,
    And sighing and kissing,
  And sighing and kissing so close.'

Cupid, in shape of a swain did appear,
He saw the sad wound, and in pity drew near;
Then showed her his arrow, and bid her not fear,
For the pain was no more than a maiden may bear.
When the balm was infused, she was not at a loss,
What they meant by their sighing and kissing so close;
    By their praying and whining,
    And clasping and twining,
    And panting and wishing,
    And sighing and kissing,
  And sighing and kissing so close.

JOHN DRYDEN

If the heart of a man

If the heart of man is depressed with cares,
The mist is dispelled when a woman appears;
Like the notes of a fiddle, she sweetly, sweetly
Raises the spirits and charms our ears
   Roses and lilies her cheeks disclose,
   But her ripe lips are more sweet than those,
   Press her,
   Caress her,
   With blisses
   Her kisses
Dissolve us in pleasure, and soft repose.

JOHN GAY

Love in Umbria

For years on my teenage bed between farm, sea and mine
    I saw through the Medici books a new life
Of grape-vines, cupolas, fig-leaves, olives and porticos,
    Ancient hill towns with garlanded white oxen
Pious and gentle, the Fonti del Clitunno
    Whose classical crystal waters bordered by
An intense green gush in a sudden flowering,
    Sloe-eyed maidens surrounded by fauns and satyrs
Bathing and splashing naked in the scented pools of love.

At twenty-one I went to that dark hilly city
    Perugia, Etruscan, Gothic, but not gay,
And on a vast sweating flea-ridden bed encountered
    My first love, blonde, blue-eyed, full-breasted, long-
        legged
Mary Manin, from Istrian Pola, famed for its Roman
    Amphitheatre and Golden Gate, who taught me
In her analytical affectionate Slav way
    That Italy was much more mountainous than
        meadow,
So Italy became my spiritual father, not my mother.

RONALD BOTTRALL

Unfelt, unheard, unseen

Unfelt, unheard, unseen,
I've left my little queen,
Her languid arms in silver slumber lying.
Ah, through their nestling touch,
Who, who could tell how much
There is for madness — cruel, or complying?

Those fairy lids how sleek!
Those lips how moist! They speak,
In ripest quiet, shadows of sweet sounds;
Into my fancy's ear
Melting a burden dear,
How 'Love doth know no fullness nor no bounds'.

True, tender monitors!
I bend unto your laws —
This sweetest day for dalliance was born!
So, without more ado,
I'll feel my heaven anew,
For all the blushing of the hasty morn.

JOHN KEATS

A Ballad of Andrew and Maudlin

Andrew and Maudlin, Rebecca and Will
   Margaret and Thomas, and Jocky and Mary,
Kate o'th' Kitchen, and Kit of the Mill,
   Dick the Ploughman, and Joan of the Dairy,
To solace their Lives, and to sweeten their Labour,
All met on a time with a Pipe and a Tabor.

Andrew was Clothed in Shepherd's Grey,
   And Will had put on his Holy-day Jacket,
Beck had a Coat of Popin-jay,
   And Madge had a Ribbon hung down to her Placket;
Megg and Moll in Frize, John and Jocky in Leather,
And so they began all to Foot it together.

Their Heads, and their Arms about them they flung,
   With all the might and force they had;
Their Legs went like Flails, and as loosely hung,
   They Cudgel'd their Arses as if they were Mad:
Their Faces did shine, and there Fires did kindle,
While the Maids they did trip and turn like a Spindle.

Andrew Chuck'd Maudlin under the Chin,
   Simper she did like a Furmity Kettle;
The twang of those blobber-lips made such a din,
   As if her Chaps had been made of Bell-mettle.
Kate laughed heartily at this same smack,
And loud she did answer it with a Bum-crack.

At no Whitsun-Ale there e'er yet had been
   Such Fraysters and Friskers as these Lads and Lasses;
From their Faces the Sweat ran down to be seen,
   But sure I am, much more from their Arses.
For had you but seen't, you then would have sworn,
You never beheld the like since you were born.

Here they did Fling, and there they did Hoist;
Here a hot Breath, and there went a Savour;
Here they did glance, and there they did gloist;
Here they did Simper, and there they did Slaver.
Here was a Hand, and there was a Placket,
Whilst, hey! their Sleeves went Flicket-a-flacket.

The Dance being ended, they sweat and they stunk.
The Maidens did smirk it, the Youngsters did Kiss 'em;
Cakes and Ale flew about, they clapp'd hands and
     drunk,
They laugh'd and they giggl'd until they Be-pist 'em.
They laid the Girls down, and gave each a green Mantle,
While their Breasts and their Bellies went a-Pintle
     a-Pantle.

THOMAS DURFEY

Come, Shepherds, Come!

Come, shepherds, come!
Come away
Without delay,
Whilst the gentle time doth stay.
Green woods are dumb,
And will never tell to any
Those dear kisses, and those many
Sweet embraces that are given;
Dainty pleasures, that would even
Raise in coldest age a fire,
And give virgin-blood desire.
Then, if ever,
Now or never,
Come and have it:
Think not I
Dare deny,
If you crave it.

JOHN FLETCHER

Lovers, Rejoice!

Lovers, rejoice! your pains shall be rewarded;
The god of love himself grieves at your crying;
No more shall frozen honour be regarded,
Nor the coy faces of a maid denying.
No more shall virgins sigh, and say 'We dare not,
For men are false, and what they do they care not.'
All shall be well again; then do not grieve;
Men shall be true, and women shall believe.

Lovers, rejoice! what you shall say henceforth,
When you have caught your sweethearts in your arms,
It shall be accounted oracle and worth;
No more faint-hearted girls shall dream of harms,
And cry they are too young; the god hath said,
Fifteen shall make a mother of a maid:
Then, wise men, pull your roses yet unblown:
Love hates the too-ripe fruit that falls alone.

FRANCIS BEAUMONT or JOHN FLETCHER

An Incomparable Kiss

Give me a kiss from those sweet lips of thine
And make it double by enjoining mine,
Another yet, nay yet and yet another,
And let the first kiss be the second's brother.
Give me a thousand kisses and yet more;
And then repeat those that have gone before;
Let us begin while daylight springs in heaven,
And kiss till night descends into the even,
And when that modest secretary, night,
Discolours all but thy heaven beaming bright,
We will begin revels of hidden love
In that sweet orb where silent pleasures move.
In high new strains, unspeakable delight,
We'll vent the dull hours of the silent night:
Were the bright day no more to visit us,
Oh, then for ever would I hold thee thus,
Naked, enchained, empty of idle fear,
As the first lovers in the garden were.
I'll die betwixt thy breasts that are so white,
For, to die there, would do a man delight.
Embrace me still, for time runs on before,
And being dead we shall embrace no more.
Let us kiss faster than the hours do fly,
Long live each kiss and never know to die.
Yet, if that fade and fly away too fast,
Impress another and renew the last;
Let us vie kisses, till our eyelids cover,
And if I sleep, count me an idle lover;
Admit I sleep, I'll still pursue the theme,
And eagerly I'll kiss thee in a dream.

Oh! give me way: grant love to me thy friend!
Did hundred thousand suitors all contend
For thy virginity, there's none shall woo
With heart so firm as mine; none better do
Than I with your sweet sweetness; if you doubt,
Pierce with your eyes my heart, or pluck it out.

ANON

Young Coridon and Phillis

Young Coridon and Phillis
  Sat in a lovely grove
Contriving crowns of lilies,
  Repeating tales of love:
And something else, but what I dare not name.

But as they were a-playing
  She ogled so the swain
It saved her plainly saying
  'Let's kiss to ease our pain:
And something else, but what I dare not name.'

A thousand times he kissed her,
  Laying her on the green,
But as he further pressed her,
  Her pretty leg was seen:
And something else, but what I dare not name.

So many beauties removing
  His ardour still increased,
And greater joys pursuing
  He wandered o'er her breast:
And something else, but what I dare not name.

A last effort she trying
  His passion to withstand,
Cried (but it was faintly crying)
  'Pray take away your hand,
And something else, but what I dare not name.'

Young Coridon grown bolder
  The minute would improve;
'This is the time', he told her,
  'To show you how I love —
And something else, but what I dare not name.'

The nymph seemed almost dying,
   Dissolved in amorous heat;
She kissed and told him sighing
   'My dear, your love is great:
And something else, but what I dare not name.'

But Phillis did recover
   Much sooner than the swain;
She blushing asked her lover
   'Shall we not kiss again,
And something else, but what I dare not name?'

Thus love his revels keeping
   Till nature at a stand
From talk they fell to sleeping,
   Holding each other's hand:
And something else, but what I dare not name.

SIR CHARLES SEDLEY

To the State of Love, or the Senses Festival

I saw a Vision yesternight
Enough to tempt a *Seekers* sight:
I wisht my self a *Shaker* there,
And her quick pulse my trembling sphere.
It was a She so glittering bright:
You'd think her soul an *Adamite*;
A person of so rare a frame,
Her body might be lin'd with 'same.
Beauties chiefest Maid of Honour:
You'd break a Lent with looking on her.
   Not the fair Abbess of the skies,
   With all her Nunnery of eyes,
   Can show me such a glorious prize.

And yet, because 'tis more renown
To make a shadow shine, she's brown:
A brown, for which Heaven would disband
The Galaxy, and stars be tann'd.
Brown by reflection, as her eye
Dazzles the Summers livery
Old dormant windows must confess
Her beams; their glimmering spectacles
Struck with the splendour of her face,
Do th'office of a burning-glass.
   Now, where such radiant lights have shown,
   No wonder if her cheeks be grown
   Sun-burnt with lustre of her own.

My sight took pay, but (thank my charms)
I now empale her in mine arms,
(Loves Compasses) confining you,
Good Angels, to a compass too.
Is not the Universe strait-lac't,
When I can clasp it in the Waste?
My amorous folds about thee hurl'd,

Adamite: nudist sectarian

43

With *Drake*, I compass in the world.
I hoop the Firmament, and make
This my Embrace the Zodiac.
　　How would thy Centre take my Sense,
　　When Admiration doth commence
　　At the extreme Circumference.

Now to the melting kiss that sips
The jelly'd Philtre of her lips,
So sweet, there is no tongue can phras't
Till transubstantiate with a taste,
Inspir'd like *Mahomet* from above,
By th'billing of my heav'nly Dove;
Love prints his Signets in her smacks,
Those Ruddy drops of squeezing wax;
Which, wheresoever she imparts,
They're Privy Seals to take up hearts.
　　Our mouths encountering at the sport,
　　My slippery soul had quit the fort,
　　But that she stopt the Sally-port.

Next to those sweets her lips dispense,
As Twin-conserves of Eloquence;
The sweet perfume her breath affords;
Incorporating with her words;
No Rosary this Votress needs,
Her very syllables are beads.
No sooner 'twixt those Rubies born:
But Jewels are in Ear-rings worn.
With what delight her speech doth enter,
It is a kiss o'th'second venter
　　And I dissolve at what I hear,
　　As if another *Rosomond* were
　　Couch'd in the Labyrinth of my Ear.

second venter: second marriage

44

Yet, that's but a preludious bliss;
Two souls pickearing in a kiss.
Embraces do but draw the Line,
'Tis storming that must take her in.
When bodies join and victory hovers
'Twixt the equal fluttering lovers
This is the game: make stakes my Dear,
Hark how the sprightly *Chanticlere*,
That Baron *Tell-clock* of the night,
Sounds Boot-esel to Cupids knight.
 Then have at all, the pass is got,
 For coming off, oh name it not:
 Who would not die upon the spot.

JOHN CLEVELAND

pickearing: skirmishing
Boot-esel: boot and saddle

may i feel said he

may i feel said he
(i'll squeal said she
just once said he)
it's fun said she

(may i touch said he
how much said she
a lot said he)
why not said she

(let's go said he
not too far said she
what's too far said he
where you are said she)

may i stay said he
(which way said she
like this said he
if you kiss said she

may i move said he
is it love said she)
if you're willing said he
(but you're killing said she

but it's life said he
but your wife said she
now said he)
ow said she

(tiptop said he
don't stop said she
oh no said he)
go slow said she

(cccome?said he
ummm said she)
you're divine!said he
(you are Mine said she)

e. e. cummings

she being Brand

she being Brand

-new;and you
know consequently a
little stiff i was
careful of her and(having

thoroughly oiled the universal
joint tested my gas felt of
her radiator made sure her springs were O.

K.)i went right to it flooded-the-carburetor cranked her

up,slipped the
clutch(and then somehow got into reverse she
kicked what
the hell)next
minute i was back in neutral tried and

again slo-wly;bare,ly nudg.   ing(my

lev-er Right-
oh and her gears being in
A 1 shape passed
from low through
second-in-to-high like
greasedlightning)just as we turned the corner of Divinity

avenue i touched the accelerator and give

her the juice, good

                    (it
was the first ride and believe i we was
happy to see how nice she acted right up to

the last minute coming back down by the Public
Gardens i slammed on
the

internalexpanding
&
externalcontracting
brakes Bothatonce and

brought allofher tremB
-ling
to a:dead.

stand-
;Still)

e. e. cummings

A Song of Dalliance

Hark, my Flora! Love doth call us
To that strife that must befall us.
He has rob'd his mother's Myrtles
And hath pull'd her downy Turtles.
See, our genial hosts are crown'd,
And our beds like billows rise:
Softer combat's nowhere found,
And who loses, wins the prize.

Let not dark nor shadows fright thee;
Thy limbs of lustre they will light thee.
Fear not any can surprise us,
Love himself doth now disguise us.
From thy waist thy girdle throw:
Night and darkness both dwell here:
Words or actions who can know,
Where there's neither eye nor ear?

Show thy bosom and then hide it;
License touching and then chide it;
Give a grant and then forbear it,
Offer something, and forswear it;
Ask where all our shame is gone;
Call us wicked wanton men;
Do as turtles, kiss and groan;
Say 'We ne'er shall meet again.'

I can hear thee curse, yet chase thee;
Drink thy tears, yet still embrace thee;
Easy riches is no treasure;
She that's willing spoils the pleasure.
Love bids learn the wrestlers' fight;
Pull and struggle whilst ye twine;
Let me use my force tonight,
The next conquest shall be thine.

WILLIAM CARTWRIGHT

I will give my love an apple

I will give my love an apple without any core,
I will give my love a house without any door.
I will give my love a palace wherein she may be,
And she may unlock it without any key.

My head is the apple without any core,
My mind is the house without any door,
My heart is the palace wherein she may be
And she may unlock it without any key.

I will give my love a cherry without any stone,
I will give my love a chick without any bone,
I will give my love a ring, not a rent to be seen,
I will get my love children without any crying.

When the cherry's in blossom there's never a stone,
When the chick's in the egg there is never a bone,
When the ring is a-running there's not a rent to be
    seen,
And when they're child-making they're seldom
    crying.

ANON

Pomona de Maillol

For Eve

An old man tamed his garden with wet clay
Until Pomona rose, a bubble in his arms.

The time and place grow ripe when the idea
Marries its proper image in volition,
When desire and intention kiss and bruise.

A cord passed round the body of the mermaid
Drew her sleeping from the underworld,
As when the breath of resin like a code
Rises from some unguarded still, Pomona
Breathing, surely a little out of breath
The image disengaging from the block,
A little out of breath, and wondering

If art is self-reflection, *who* he was
She woke within the side of, *what* old man
In his smock and dirty cap of cloth,
Drinking through trembling fingers now
A ten year siege of her, the joy in touching
The moistened flanks of her idea with all
An old man's impatience of the carnal wish?

LAWRENCE DURRELL

The Gordian Knot

The Gordian knot, which Alexander great
　　Did whilom cut with his all-conquering sword,
Was nothing like thy busk-point, pretty peat,
　　Nor could so fair an augury afford;
Which if I chance to cut or else untie,
Thy little world I'll conquer presently.

THOMAS TOMKISS?

I have a gentle cock

I have a gentle cock
　Croweth me day;
He doth me risen early
　My matins for to say.

I have a gentle cock;
　Comen he is of great;
His comb is of red coral,
　His tail is of jet.

I have a gentle cock;
　Comen he is of kind;
His comb is of red coral,
　His tail is of ind.

His leggës are of azure,
　So gentle and so small;
His spurs are of silver white
　Into the wortëwale.

His eyes are of crystal
　Locked all in amber;
And every night he percheth him
　In my lady's chamber.

ANON

Comen he is of great: come from a noble line
ind: indigo
wortëwale: skin of the claws

Enjoyment

In the Dark None Dainty

Night hides our thefts; all faults then pardoned be:
All are alike fair when no spots we see.
Lais and Lucretia in the night-time are
Pleasing alike; alike both singular:
Joan and my lady have at that time one,
One and the self-same prized complexion.
Then please alike the pewter and the plate,
The chosen ruby and the reprobate.

ROBERT HERRICK

Begging Another,
On Colour of Mending the Former

For Love's sake, kiss me once again,
I long, and should not beg in vain.
    Here's none to spy or see;
        Why do you doubt or stay?
    I'll taste as lightly as the bee,
That doth but touch his flower, and flies
        away.

Once more, and, faith, I will be gone,
Can he that loves ask less than one?
    Nay, you may err in this,
        And all your bounty wrong:
    This could be called but half a kiss;
What we're but once to do, we should do
        long.

I will but mend the last, and tell
Where, how, it would have relished well;
    Join lip to lip, and try:
        Each suck the other's breath,
    And whilst our tongues perplexed lie,
Let who will think us dead, or wish our
        death.

BEN JONSON

White Heliotrope

The feverish room and that white bed,
The tumbled skirts upon a chair,
The novel flung half-open, where
Hat, hair-pins, puffs, and paints, are spread;

The mirror that has sucked your face
Into its secret deep of deeps,
And there mysteriously keeps
Forgotten memories of grace;

And you, half dressed and half awake,
Your slant eyes strangely watching me,
And I, who watch you drowsily,
With eyes that, having slept not, ache;

This (need one dread? nay, dare one hope?)
Will rise, a ghost of memory, if
Ever again my handkerchief
Is scented with White Heliotrope.

ARTHUR SYMONS

Over the hill and over the dale

Over the hill and over the dale,
And over the bourn to Dawlish,
Where gingerbread wives have a scanty sale
And gingerbread nuts are smallish.

Rantipole Betty she ran down a hill,
And kicked up her petticoats fairly.
Says I, 'I'll be Jack if you will be Jill.'
So she sat on the grass debonairly.

'Here's somebody coming, here's somebody coming!'
Says I, ''Tis the wind at a parley.'
So without any fuss, any hawing and humming,
She lay on the grass debonairly.

'Here's somebody here and here's somebody *there*!'
Says I, 'Hold your tongue you young gipsy.'
So she held her tongue and lay plump and fair
And dead as a Venus tipsy.

Oh, who wouldn't hie to Dawlish fair,
Oh, who wouldn't stop in a meadow?
Oh, who would not rumple the daisies there
And make the wild fern for a bed do?

JOHN KEATS

Hush, hush! Tread softly!
Hush, hush, my dear!

I

Hush, hush! Tread softly! Hush, hush, my dear!
All the house is asleep, but we know very well
That the jealous, the jealous old bald-pate may hear,
  Though you've padded his night-cap, O sweet Isabel!
  Though your feet are more light than a fairy's feet,
  Who dances on bubbles where brooklets meet.
Hush, hush! Soft tiptoe! Hush, hush my dear!
For less than a nothing the jealous can hear.

II

No leaf doth tremble, no ripple is there
  On the river; all's still, and the night's sleepy eye
Closes up, and forgets all its Lethean care,
  Charmed to death by the drone of the humming
      mayfly;
  And the moon, whether prudish or complaisant,
  Has fled to her bower, well knowing I want
No light in the dusk, no torch in the gloom,
But my Isabel's eyes, and her lips pulped with bloom.

III

Lift the latch! Ah, gently! Ah, tenderly, sweet!
  We are dead if that latchet gives one little clink —
Well done — now those lips, and a flowery seat;
  The old man may sleep, and the planets may wink!
  The shut rose shall dream of our loves and awake
  Full blown, and such warmth for the morning's take;
The stock-dove shall hatch her soft brace and shall coo,
While I kiss to the melody, aching all through!

JOHN KEATS

59

Roundelay

1

Chloe found Amyntas lying,
  All in tears, upon the plain,
Sighing to himself, and crying,
  'Wretched I, to love in vain!
'Kiss me, dear, before my dying;
  'Kiss me once, and ease my pain.'

2

Sighing to himself, and crying,
  'Wretched I, to love in vain!
'Ever scorning, and denying
  'To reward your faithful swain:
'Kiss me, dear, before my dying;
  'Kiss me once, and ease my pain!

3

'Ever scorning, and denying
  'To reward your faithful swain.'
Chloe, laughing at his crying,
  Told him, that he loved in vain.
'Kiss me, dear, before my dying;
  'Kiss me once, and ease my pain!'

4

Chloe, laughing at his crying,
  Told him that he loved in vain;
But repenting, and complying,
  When he kissed, she kissed again:
Kissed him up before his dying;
  Kissed him up, and eased his pain.

JOHN DRYDEN

Up Tailes All

Begin with a kisse,
Go on too with this:
And thus, thus, thus let us smother
Our lips for a while,
But let's not beguile
Our hope of one for the other.

This play, be assur'd,
Long enough has endur'd,
Since more and more is exacted;
For love he doth call
For his Uptailes all;
And that's the part to be acted.

ROBERT HERRICK

The Comparison

As the sweet sweat of roses in a still,
As that which from chafed musk cat's pores doth trill,
As the almighty balm of th' early east,
Such are the sweat drops of my mistress' breast.
And on her neck her skin such lustre sets,
They seem no sweat drops, but pearl carcanets.
Rank sweaty froth thy mistress' brow defiles,
Like spermatic issue of ripe menstruous boils,
Or like that scum, which, by need's lawless law
Enforced, Sanserra's starved men did draw
From parboiled shoes, and boots, and all the rest
Which were with any sovereign fatness blessed,
And like vile lying stones in saffroned tin,
Or warts, or weals, they hang upon her skin.
Round as the world's her head, on every side,
Like to the fatal ball which fell on Ide,
Or that whereof God had such jealousy,
As for the ravishing thereof we die.
Thy head is like a rough-hewn statue of jet,
Where marks for eyes, nose, mouth, are yet scarce set;
Like the first Chaos, or flat seeming face
Of Cynthia, when th' earth's shadows her embrace.
Like Proserpine's white beauty-keeping chest,
Or Jove's best fortune's urn, is her fair breast.
Thine's like worm-eaten trunks, clothed in seal's skin,
Or grave, that's dust without, and stink within.
And like that slender stalk, at whose end stands
The woodbine quivering, are her arms and hands.
Like rough-barked elmboughs, or the russet skin
Of men late scourged for madness, or for sin,
Like sun-parched quarters on the city gate,
Such is thy tanned skin's lamentable state.
And like a bunch of ragged carrots stand
The short swoll'n fingers of thy gouty hand.
Then like the chemic's masculine equal fire,

Enjoyment

Which in the limbeck's warm womb doth inspire
Into th' earth's worthless dirt a soul of gold,
Such cherishing heat her best loved part doth hold.
Thine's like the dread mouth of a fired gun,
Or like hot liquid metals newly run
Into clay moulds, or like to that Etna
Where round about the grass is burnt away.
Are not your kisses then as filthy, and more,
As a worm sucking an envenomed sore?
Doth not thy fearful hand in feeling quake,
As one which gathering flowers, still fears a snake?
Is not your last act harsh, and violent,
As when a plough a stony ground doth rent?
So kiss good turtles, so devoutly nice
Are priests in handling reverent sacrifice,
And such in searching wounds the surgeon is
As we, when we embrace, or touch, or kiss.
Leave her, and I will leave comparing thus,
She, and comparisons are odious.

JOHN DONNE

Incident in a Life

On a heath in Dorset
Car parked by the road.
They wanted it,
Have had it, and that's that.

And comically — laugh, go on —
His damp foreskin balloons
Lopsidedly,
Having been bitten
Before or after by a gnat.

GEOFFREY GRIGSON

THE ONE AND ONLY

Part of Plenty

When she carries food to the table and stoops down
— Doing this out of love — and lays soup with its good
Tickling smell, or fry winking from the fire
And I look up, perhaps from a book I am reading
Or other work: there is an importance of beauty
Which can't be accounted for by there and then,
And attacks me, but not separately from the welcome
Of the food, or the grace of her arms.

When she puts a sheaf of tulips in a jug
And pours in water and presses to one side
The upright stems and leaves that you hear creak,
Or loosens them, or holds them up to show me,
So that I see the tangle of their necks and cups
With the curls of her hair, and the body they are held
Against, and the stalk of the small waist rising
And flowering in the shape of breasts;

Whether in the bringing of the flowers or the food
She offers plenty, and is part of plenty,
And whether I see her stooping, or leaning with the
        flowers,
What she does is ages old, and she is not simply,
No, but lovely in that way.

BERNARD SPENCER

A Description

I sing her worth and praises high,
Of whom a poet cannot lie.
The little world the great shall blaze:
Sea, earth her body; heaven her face;
Her hair sunbeams, whose every part
Lightens, inflames each lover's heart,
That thus you prove the axiom true,
Whilst the sun help'd nature in you.

Her front the white and azure sky,
In light and glory raised high;
Being o'ercast by a cloudy frown,
All hearts and eyes dejecteth down.

Her each brow a celestial bow,
Which through this sky her light doth show,
Which doubled, if it strange appear,
The sun's likewise is doubled there.

Her either cheek a blushing morn,
Which, on the wings of beauty borne,
Doth never set, but only fair
Shineth, exalted in her hair.

Within her mouth, heaven's heav'n, reside
Her words: the soul's there glorifi'd.

Her nose th' equator of this globe,
Where nakedness, beauty's best robe,
Presents a form all hearts to win.

Last Nature made that dainty chin,
Which, that it might in every fashion
Answer the rest, a constellation,
Like to a desk, she there did place
To write the wonders of her face.

In this celestial frontispiece,
Where happiness eternal lies,
First arranged stand three senses,
This heaven's intelligences,
Whose several motions, sweet combin'd,
Come from the first mover, her mind.

The One and Only

The weight of this harmonic sphere
The Atlas of her neck doth bear,
Whose favours day to us imparts,
When frowns make night in lovers' hearts.
Two foaming billows are her breasts,
That carry rais'd upon their crests
The Tyrian fish: more white 's their foam
Than that whence Venus once did come.
Here take her by the hand, my Muse,
With that sweet foe to make my truce,
To compact manna best compar'd,
Whose dewy inside 's not full hard.
Her waist 's an invers'd pyramis,
Upon whose cone love's trophy is.
Her belly is that magazine
At whose peep Nature did resign
That precious mould by which alone
There can be framed such a one.
At th' entrance of which hidden treasure,
Happy making above measure,
Two alabaster pillars stand,
To warn all passage from that land;
At foot whereof engraved is
The sad *Non ultra* of man's bliss.
The back of this most precious frame
Holds up in majesty the same,
Where, to make music to all hearts,
Love bound the descant of her parts.
Though all this Beauty's temple be,
There 's known within no deity
Save virtues shrin'd within her will.
As I began, so say I still,
I sing her worth and praises high,
Of whom a poet cannot lie.

LORD HERBERT OF CHERBURY

The Gowden Locks of Anna

Yestreen I had a pint o' wine,
  A place where body saw na;
Yestreen lay on this breast o' mine
  The gowden locks of Anna.

The hungry Jew in wilderness,
  Rejoicing o'er his manna,
Was naething to my hinnie bliss
  Upon the lips of Anna.

Ye monarchs, take the East and West
  Frae Indus to Savannah;
Gie me, within my straining grasp,
  The melting form of Anna.

There I'll despise Imperial charms,
  An Empress or Sultana,
While dying raptures in her arms
  I give and take wi' Anna!

Awa, thou flaunting God of Day!
  Awa, thou pale Diana!
Ilk Star, gae hide thy twinkling ray,
  When I'm to meet my Anna!

Come, in thy raven plumage, Night,
  (Sun, Moon, and Stars, withdrawn a';)
And bring an angel-pen to write
  My transports with my Anna!

POSTSCRIPT
The Kirk an' State may join, an' tell
  To do sic things I maunna:
The Kirk an' State may go to hell,
  An I'll gae to my Anna.

The One and Only

She is the sunshine o' my e'e,
  To live but here I canna;
Had I on earth but wishes three,
  The first should be my Anna.

ROBERT BURNS

Fair is my Love

Fair is my Love that feeds among the lilies,
The lilies growing in that pleasant garden
Where Cupid's Mount that well beloved hill is,
And where that little god himself is warden.
See where my Love sits in the beds of spices,
Beset all round with camphor, myrrh, and roses,
And interlaced with curious devices
Which her apart from all the world encloses!
There doth she tune her lute for her delight,
And with sweet music makes the ground to move,
Whilst I, poor I, do sit in heavy plight,
Wailing alone my unrespected love;
   Not daring rush into so rare a place,
   That gives to her, and she to it, a grace.

BARTHOLOMEW GRIFFIN

The Woman

I have never
clearly given to you
the associations
you have for me, you

with such
divided presence my dream
does not show
you. I do not dream.

I have compounded
these sensations, the
accumulation of the things
left me by you.

Always your
tits, not breasts, but
harsh sudden rises
of impatient flesh

on the chest — is it
mine — which flower
against the vagueness
of the air you move in.

You walk
such a shortness
of intent strides, your
height is so low,

in my hand
I feel the weight
of yours there,
one over one

or both, as you
pivot upon me, the
same weight grown
as the hair, the

second of your attributes,
falls to
cover us. We
couple but lie against

no surface, have
lifted as you again
grow small
against myself, into

the air. The
air the third of
the signs you
are known by: a

quiet, a
soughing silence,
the winds lightly
moved. Then

your
mouth, it
opens not
speaking, touches,

wet, on me. Then
I scream, I
sing such as is
given to me, roar-

The One and Only

ing unheard,
like stark sight
sees itself
inverted

into dark
turned. Onanistic,
I feel around
myself what

you have left me
with, wetness, pools
of it, my skin
drips.

ROBERT CREELEY

The Complement

O my dearest, I shall grieve thee,
When I swear (yet, sweet, believe me,)
By thine eyes, the tempting book
On which even crabb'd old men look,
I swear to thee, though none abhor them,
Yet I do not love thee for them.

I do not love thee for that fair
Rich fan of thy most curious hair;
Though the wires thereof be drawn
Finer than the threads of lawn,
And are softer than the leaves
On which the subtle spinner weaves.

I do not love thee for those flowers
Growing on thy cheeks (Love's bowers);
Though such cunning them hath spread,
None can paint their white and red;
Love's golden arrows thence are shot,
Yet for them I love thee not.

I do not love thee for those soft
Red coral lips I've kiss'd so oft;
Nor teeth of pearl, the double guard
To speech, whence music still is heard;
Though from those lips a kiss being taken
Might tyrants melt, and death awaken.

I do not love thee, O my fairest!
For that richest, for that rarest
Silver pillar which stands under
Thy sound head, that globe of wonder;
Though that neck be whiter far
Than towers of polish'd ivory are.

The One and Only

I do not love thee for those mountains
Hill'd with snow, whence milky fountains
(Sugar'd sweets, as syrup'd berries),
Must one day run through pipes of cherries:
O how much those breasts do move me!
Yet for them I do not love thee.

I do not love thee for that belly,
Sleek as satin, soft as jelly;
Though within that crystal round
Heaps of treasure might be found,
So rich, that for the best of them
A king might leave his diadem.

I do not love thee for those thighs,
Whose alabaster rocks do rise
So high and even, that they stand
Like sea-marks to some happy land:
Happy are those eyes have seen them,
More happy they that sail between them.

I love thee not for thy moist palm,
Though the dew thereof be balm;
Nor for thy pretty leg and foot,
Although it be the precious root,
On which this goodly cedar grows:
Sweet, I love thee not for those.

Nor for thy wit, though pure and quick,
Whose substance no arithmetic
Can number down; nor for those charms
Mask'd in thy embracing arms,
Though in them one night to lie,
Dearest, I would gladly die.

From Bed to Verse

I love not for those eyes, nor hair,
Nor cheeks, nor lips, nor teeth so rare,
Nor for thy speech, thy neck, nor breast,
Nor for thy belly, nor the rest,
Nor for thy hand nor foot so small:
But, wouldst thou know, dear sweet, for all.

THOMAS CAREW

A Rapture

I will enjoy thee now, my Celia, come,
And fly with me to Love's Elysium.
The giant, Honour, that keeps cowards out,
Is but a masquer, and the servile rout
Of baser subjects only bend in vain
To the vast idol; whilst the nobler train
Of valiant lovers daily sail between
The huge Colossus' legs, and pass unseen
Unto the blissful shore. Be bold and wise,
And we shall enter: the grim Swiss denies
Only to tame fools a passage, that not know
He is but form and only frights in show
The duller eyes that look from far; draw near
And thou shalt scorn what we were wont to fear.
We shall see how the stalking pageant goes
With borrow'd legs, a heavy load to those
That made and bear him; not, as we once thought
The seed of gods, but a weak model wrought
By greedy men, that seek to enclose the common,
And within private arms empale free woman.
    Come, then, and mounted on the wings of Love
We'll cut the flitting air and soar above
The monster's head, and in the noblest seats
Of those blest shades quench and renew our heats.
There shall the queens of love and innocence,
Beauty and Nature, banish all offence
From our close ivy-twines; there I'll behold
Thy bared snow and thy unbraided gold;
There my enfranchised hand on every side
Shall o'er thy naked polish'd ivory slide.
No curtain there, though of transparent lawn,
Shall be before thy virgin-treasure drawn;
But the rich mine, to the enquiring eye
Exposed, shall ready still for mintage lie,
And we will coin young Cupids. There a bed

Of roses and fresh myrtles shall be spread,
Under the cooler shade of cypress groves;
Our pillows of the down of Venus' doves,
Whereon our panting limbs we'll gently lay,
In the faint respites of our active play:
That so our slumbers may in dreams have leisure
To tell the nimble fancy our past pleasure,
And so our souls, that cannot be embraced,
Shall the embraces of our bodies taste.
Meanwhile the bubbling stream shall court the shore,
Th' enamour'd chirping wood-choir shall adore
In varied tunes the deity of love;
The gentle blasts of western winds shall move
The trembling leaves, and through their close boughs
    breathe
Still music, whilst we rest ourselves beneath
Their dancing shade; till a soft murmur, sent
From souls entranced in amorous languishment,
Rouse us, and shoot into our veins fresh fire,
Till we in their sweet ecstasy expire.
    Then, as the empty bee that lately bore
Into the common treasure all her store,
Flies 'bout the painted field with nimble wing,
Deflow'ring the fresh virgins of the spring,
So will I rifle all the sweets that dwell
In my delicious paradise, and swell
My bag with honey, drawn forth by the power
Of fervent kisses from each spicy flower.
I'll seize the rose-buds in their perfumed bed,
The violet knots, like curious mazes spread
O'er all the garden, taste the ripen'd cherry,
The warm firm apple, tipp'd with coral berry:
Then will I visit with a wand'ring kiss
The vale of lilies and the bower of bliss;
And where the beauteous region doth divide

Into two milky ways, my lips shall slide
Down those smooth alleys, wearing as they go
A tract for lovers on the printed snow;
Thence climbing o'er the swelling Apennine,
Retire into thy grove of eglantine,
Where I will all those ravish'd sweets distil
Through Love's alembic, and with chemic skill
From the mix'd mass one sovereign balm derive,
Then bring that great elixir to thy hive.
  Now in more subtle wreaths I will entwine
My sinewy thighs, my legs and arms with thine;
Thou like a sea of milk shalt lie display'd,
Whilst I the smooth calm ocean invade
With such a tempest, as when Jove of old
Fell down on Danaë in a storm of gold;
Yet my tall pine shall in the Cyprian strait
Ride safe at anchor and unlade her freight:
My rudder with thy bold hand, like a tried
And skilful pilot, thou shalt steer, and guide
My bark into love's channel, where it shall
Dance, as the bounding waves do rise or fall.
Then shall thy circling arms embrace and clip
My willing body, and thy balmy lip
Bathe me in juice of kisses, whose perfume
Like a religious incense shall consume,
And send up holy vapours to those powers
That bless our loves and crown our sportful hours,
That with such halcyon calmness fix our souls
In steadfast peace, as no affright controls.
There, no rude sounds shake us with sudden starts;
No jealous ears, when we unrip our hearts,
Suck our discourse in; no observing spies
This blush, that glance traduce; no envious eyes
Watch our close meetings; nor are we betray'd
To rivals by the bribed chambermaid.

81

No wedlock bonds unwreathe our twisted loves,
We seek no midnight arbour, no dark groves
To hide our kisses: there, the hated name
Of husband, wife, lust, modest, chaste or shame,
Are vain and empty words, whose very sound
Was never heard in the Elysian ground.
All things are lawful there, that may delight
Nature or unrestrained appetite;
Like and enjoy, to will and act is one:
We only sin when Love's rites are not done.
   The Roman Lucrece there reads the divine
Lectures of love's great master, Aretine,
And knows as well as Lais how to move
Her pliant body in the act of love;
To quench the burning ravisher she hurls
Her limbs into a thousand winding curls,
And studies artful postures, such as be
Carved on the bark of every neighbouring tree
By learned hands, that so adorn'd the rind
Of those fair plants, which, as they lay entwined,
Have fann'd their glowing fires. The Grecian dame,
That in her endless web toil'd for a name
As fruitless as her work, doth there display
Herself before the youth of Ithaca,
And th' amorous sport of gamesome nights prefer
Before dull dreams of the lost traveller.
Daphne hath broke her bark, and that swift foot
Which th' angry gods had fasten'd with a root
To the fix'd earth, doth now unfetter'd run
To meet th' embraces of the youthful Sun.
She hangs upon him like his Delphic lyre;
Her kisses blow the old, and breathe new fire;
Full of her god, she sings inspired lays,
Sweet odes of love, such as deserve the bays,
Which she herself was. Next her, Laura lies

In Petrarch's learned arms, drying those eyes
That did in such sweet smooth-paced numbers flow,
As made the world enamour'd of his woe.
These, and ten thousand beauties more, that died
Slave to the tyrant, now enlarged deride
His cancell'd laws, and for their time mis-spent
Pay into Love's exchequer double rent.
    Come then, my Celia, we'll no more forbear
To taste our joys, struck with a panic fear,
But will depose from his imperious sway
This proud usurper, and walk free as they,
With necks unyoked; nor is it just that he
Should fetter your soft sex with chastity,
Whom Nature made unapt for abstinence;
When yet this false impostor can dispense
With human justice and with sacred right,
And, maugre both their laws, command me fight
With rivals or with emulous loves that dare
Equal with thine their mistress' eyes or hair.
If thou complain of wrong, and call my sword
To carve out thy revenge, upon that word
He bids me fight and kill; or else he brands
With marks of infamy my coward hands.
And yet religion bids from blood-shed fly,
And damns me for that act. Then tell me why
    This goblin Honour, which the world adores,
    Should make men atheists, and not women whores?

THOMAS CAREW

The Second Rapture

No, worldling, no, 'tis not thy gold,
Which thou dost use but to behold,
Nor fortune, honour, nor long life,
Children, or friends, nor a good wife,
That makes thee happy: these things be
But shadows of felicity.
Give me a wench about thirteen,
Already voted to the queen
Of lust and lovers; whose soft hair
Fann'd with the breath of gentle air,
O'er-spreads her shoulders like a tent,
And is her veil and ornament;
Whose tender touch will make the blood
Wild in the aged and the good;
Whose kisses, fasten'd to the mouth
Of three-score years and longer slouth,
Renew the age; and whose bright eye
Obscures those lesser lights of sky;
Whose snowy breasts (if we may call
That snow, that never melts at all,)
Makes Jove invent a new disguise,
In spite of Juno's jealousies;
Whose every part doth re-invite
The old decayed appetite;
And in whose sweet embraces I
May melt my self to lust, and die,
  This is true bliss, and I confess
  There is no other happiness.

THOMAS CAREW

Nae Hair on't

Yestreen I wed a lady fair,
  An ye wad believe me,
On her c — t there grows nae hair,
  That's the thing that grieves me.

It vexed me sair, it plagu'd me sair,
  It put me in a passion,
To think that I had wad a wife,
  Whase c — t was out o' fashion.

ANON/ROBERT BURNS

There's Hair on't

O, ere yestreen I stented graith,
  An' labor'd lang an' sair on't;
But fient a work, na work wad it,
  There's sic a crap o' hair on't.

    There's hair on't, there's hair on't,
    There's thretty thrave an' mair on't;
    But gin I live to anither year,
    I'll tether my grey naigs on't.

An' up the glen there rase a knowe,
  Below the knowe a lair on't,
I maist had perish'd, fit an' horse,
  I could na see for hair on't.

But I'll plant a stake into the flowe,
  That ploughmen may tak care on't;
An' lay twa steppin'-stanes below,
  An' syne I'll cowe the hair on't.

ANON/ROBERT BURNS

86

The One and Only

My mistress' eyes are nothing like the sun

My mistress' eyes are nothing like the sun;
Coral is far more red than her lips' red;
If snow be white, why then her breasts are dun;
If hairs be wires, black wires grow on her head.
I have seen roses damask'd, red and white,
But no such roses see I in her cheeks;
And in some perfumes is there more delight
Than in the breath that from my mistress reeks.
I love to hear her speak; yet well I know
That music hath a far more pleasing sound.
I grant I never saw a goddess go:
My mistress, when she walks, treads on the
    ground.
  And yet, by heaven, I think my love as rare
  As any she belied with false compare.

WILLIAM SHAKESPEARE

Her Triumph

See the chariot at hand here of Love,
   Wherein my Lady rideth!
Each that draws is a swan or a dove,
   And well the car Love guideth.
As she goes, all hearts do duty
    Unto her beauty;
And enamoured do wish, so they might
    But enjoy such a sight,
That they still were to run by her side,
Through swords, through seas, whither she
    would ride.

Do but look on her eyes, they do light
   All that Love's world compriseth!
Do but look on her hair, it is bright
   As Love's star when it riseth!
Do but mark, her forehead's smoother
    Than words that soothe her:
And from her arched brows, such a grace
    Sheds itself through the face,
As alone there triumphs to the life
All the gain, all the good of the elements' strife.

Have you seen but a bright lily grow,
   Before rude hands have touched it?
Have you marked but the fall o' the snow
   Before the soil hath smutched it?
Have you felt the wool of beaver?
    Or swan's down ever?
Or have smelt o' the bud o' the brier?
    Or the nard in the fire?
Or have tasted the bag of the bee?
O so white! O so soft! O so sweet is she!

BEN JONSON

The Theology of Fitness

This is what I call mind:
Your behind,
That patch of hair in front,
Your navel, your cunt,
Your nipples, your lips;
The hair in your arm-pits
(If a depilatory
Have rased that memory
The hair on your head
Will do instead).
Starting at the nape
I examine your shape;
It is intellectual
And accordingly small.
There is the line
As I descend your spine
To your two legs
Split like a clothes peg.
Quelle heureuse pensée!
You will probably say
If I want a ewe to tup
I should start higher up
And, for example, surprise
Your intellect in your eyes.
Wishing merely to understand,
Lady, I kiss your hand.

Consider, since that is you
Who I am, who
Address these courtesies
And seek to please.
Shall I admit my mind
Starts in my behind
Or that my balls and hair
Gives my verse its air?

(Less pleasant to dwell upon
I find, it is all one.)
This is my fund of wit
And cavity for shit.
Oh, there is much else
Still, when I see myself
I do not over-emphasise
The intelligence of my eyes.

So, when we resurrect
That which was once erect
(Although, in paradise
The suits are without flies)
Your spirit and your bum
Will certainly be one;
Every orifice
Will receive a kiss;
The lowly heart
Will trumpet out a fart;
There will be hosannas
From long bananas.

That being so
What shall we do now?

C. H. SISSON

COUNSEL

Against Fruition

Stay here, fond youth, and ask no more; be wise:
Knowing too much long since lost paradise.
The virtuous joys thou hast, thou wouldst should still
Last in their pride; and wouldst not take it ill,
If rudely from sweet dreams (and for a toy)
Thou wert wak'd? he wakes himself, that does enjoy.

Fruition adds no new wealth, but destroys,
And while it pleaseth much the palate, cloys;
Who thinks he shall be happier for that,
As reasonably might hope he might grow fat
By eating to a surfeit; this once past,
What relishes? even kisses lose their taste.

Urge not 'tis necessary: alas! we know
The homeliest thing which mankind does is so;
The world is of a vast extent, we see,
And must be peopled; children there must be;
So must bread too; but since they are enough
Born to the drudgery, what need we plough?

Women enjoy'd (whate'er before th' have been)
Are like romances read, or sights once seen;
Fruition 's dull, and spoils the play much more
Than if one read or knew the plot before;
'Tis expectation makes a blessing dear,
Heaven were not heaven, if we knew what it were.

And as in prospects we are there pleas'd most,
Where something keeps the eye from being lost,
And leaves us room to guess; so here restraint
Holds up delight, that with excess would faint.
They who know all the wealth they have are poor;
He's only rich that cannot tell his store.

SIR JOHN SUCKLING

The Deformed Mistress

I know there are some fools that care
Not for the body, so the face be fair;
Some others, too, that in a female creature
Respect not beauty, but a comely feature;
And others, too, that for those parts in sight
Care not so much, so that the rest be right.
Each man his humour hath, and, faith, 'tis mine
To love that woman which I now define.
First I would have her wainscot foot and hand
More wrinkled far than any pleated band,
That in those furrows, if I' d take the pains,
I might both sow and reap all sorts of grains:
Her nose I 'd have a foot long, not above,
With pimples embroider'd, for those I love;
And at the end a comely pearl of snot,
Considering whether it should fall or not:
Provided, next, that half her teeth be out,
Nor do I care much if her pretty snout
Meet with her furrow'd chin, and both together
Hem in her lips, as dry as good whit-leather:
One wall-eye she shall have, for that 's a sign
In other beasts the best: why not in mine?
Her neck I 'll have to be pure jet at least,
With yellow spots enamell'd; and her breast,
Like a grasshopper's wing, both thin and lean,
Not to be touch'd for dirt, unless swept clean:
As for her belly, 'tis no matter, so
There be a belly, and —
Yet if you will, let it be something high,
And always let there be a tympany.
But soft! where am I now? here I should stride,
Lest I fall in, the place must be so wide,
And pass unto her thighs, which shall be just
Like to an ant's that 's scraping in the dust.
Into her legs I 'd have love's issues fall,

94

And all her calf into a gouty small:
Her feet both thick and eagle-like display'd,
The symptoms of a comely, handsome maid.
As for her parts behind, I ask no more:
If they but answer those that are before,
I have my utmost wish; and, having so,
Judge whether I am happy, yea or no.

SIR JOHN SUCKLING

An Elegy

Love, give me leave to serve thee, and be wise,
To keep thy torch in, but restore blind eyes.
I will a flame into my bosom take,
That Martyrs Court when they embrace the stake:
Not dull, and smoky fires, but heat divine,
That burns not to consume, but to refine.
I have a Mistress for perfections rare
In every eye, but in my thoughts most fair.
Like Tapers on the Altar shine her eyes;
Her breath is the perfume of Sacrifice.
And whereso'ere my fancy would begin,
Still her perfection lets religion in.
I touch her like my Beads with devout care;
And come unto my Courtship as my Prayer.
We sit, and talk, and kiss away the hours,
As chastely as the morning dews kiss flowers.
Go wanton Lover spare thy sighs and tears,
Put on the Livery which thy dotage wears,
And call it Love, where heresy gets in
Zeal's but a coal to kindle greater sin.
We wear no flesh, but one another greet,
As blessed souls in separation meet.
Were't possible that my ambitious sin,
Durst commit rapes upon a *Cherubin*,
I might have lustful thoughts to her, of all
Earths heav'nly Quire, the most Angelical.
Looking into my breast, her form I find
That like my Guardian-Angel keeps my mind
From rude attempts; and when affections stir,
I calm all passions with one thought of her.

Thus they whose reasons love, and not their sense,
The spirits love: thus one Intelligence
Reflects upon his like, and by chaste loves
In the same sphere this and that Angel moves.

Counsel

Nor is this barren Love; one noble thought
Begets an other, and that still is brought
To bed of more; virtues and grace increase,
And such a numerous issue ne're can cease.
Where Children, though great blessings, only be
Pleasures repriev'd to some posterity.
Beasts love like men, if men in lust delight,
And call that Love which is but appetite.
When essence meets with essence, and souls join
In mutual knots, that's the true Nuptial twine:
Such Lady is my Love, and such is true;
All other Love is to your Sex, not You.

THOMAS RANDOLPH

Beauty and Denial

No, no, it cannot be; for who e'r set
A Blockhouse to defend a Garden yet?
Roses ne'r chide my boldness when I go
To crop their Blush; why should your Cheeks do so?
The Lilies ne'r deny their Silk to men;
Why should your Hands push off, and draw back then?
The Sun forbids me not his Heat; then why
Comes there to Earth an Edict from your Eye?
I smell Perfumes, and they ne'r think it sin;
Why should your Breath not let me take it in?
A Dragon kept the Golden Apples; true;
But must your Breasts be therefore kept so too?
All Fountains else flow freely, and ne'r shrink;
And must yours cheat my Thirst when I would drink?
Where Nature knows no prohibition,
Shall Art prove Anti-Nature, and make one?
   But O we scorn the proffer'd Lip and Face;
And angry Frowns sometimes add quicker Grace
Then quiet Beauty: 'tis that melting kiss
That truly doth distil immortal Bliss
Which the fierce struggling Youth by force at length
Doth make the purchase of his eager strength;
Which, from the rifled weeping Virgin scant
Snatch'd, proves a Conquest, rather than a Grant.
   Believe't not: 'tis the Paradox of some One,
That in Old time did love an Amazon,
One of so stiff a Temper, that she might
Have call'd him Spouse upon the Marriage night;
Whose Flames consum'd him lest some one might be
Seduc'd hereafter by his Heresy:
   That you are Fair and spotless, makes you prove
Fitter to fall a Sacrifice to Love:
Oh tow'rds his Altar then, vext not the Priest;
'Tis Ominous if the Sacrifice resist.
Who conquers still, and ransacks, we may say

Doth not Affect, but rather is in Pay.
But if there must be a real Lists of Love,
And our Embracing a true wrestling prove,
Bare, and Anoint you then: for, if you'll do
As Wrestlers use, you must be naked too.

WILLIAM CARTWRIGHT

No Platonic Love

Tell me no more of minds embracing minds,
    And hearts exchang'd for hearts;
That Spirits Spirits meet, as Winds do Winds,
    And mix their subt'lest parts;
That two unbodi'd Essences may kiss,
And then like Angels, twist and feel one Bliss.

I was that silly thing that once was wrought
    To practise this thin Love;
I climb'd from Sex to Soul, from Soul to Thought;
    But thinking there to move,
Headlong, I roll'd from Thought to Soul, and then
From Soul I lighted at the Sex again.

As some strict down-look'd men pretend to fast
    Who yet in Closets Eat;
So Lovers who profess they Spirits taste,
    Feed yet on grosser meat;

I know they boast they Souls to Souls Convey,
How e'r they meet, the Body is the Way.
Come, I will undeceive thee, they that tread
    Those vain Aerial ways,
Are like young Heirs, and Alchemists misled
    To waste their wealth and Days,
For searching thus to be for ever Rich,
They only find a Med'cine for the Itch.

WILLIAM CARTWRIGHT

Good Counsel to a Young Maid

Gaze not on thy beauty's pride,
Tender maid, in the false tide
That from lovers' eyes doth slide.

Let thy faithful crystal show,
How thy colours come and go,
Beauties take a foil from woe.

Love, that in those smooth streams lies,
Under pity's fair disguise,
Will thy melting heart surprise.

Nets, of passion's finest thread,
Snaring poems, will be spread
All, to catch thy maidenhead.

Then beware, for those that cure
Love's disease, themselves endure
For reward a calenture.

Rather let the lover pine,
Than his pale cheek should assign
A perpetual blush to thine.

THOMAS CAREW

calenture: deluding dream

Epode

Not to know vice at all, and keep true state,
  Is virtue and not Fate:
Next to that virtue, is to know vice well,
  And her black spite expel.
Which to effect (since no breast is so sure,
  Or safe, but she'll procure
Some way of entrance) we must plant a guard
  Of thoughts to watch and ward
At the eye and ear, the ports unto the mind,
  That no strange or unkind
Object arrive there, but the heart, our spy,
  Give knowledge instantly,
To wakeful reason, our affections' king:
  Who, in th' examining,
Will quickly taste the treason, and commit
  Close, the close cause of it.
'Tis the securest policy we have,
  To make our sense our slave.
But this true course is not embraced by many:
  By many! scarce by any.
For either our affections do rebel,
  Or else the sentinel,
That should ring larum to the heart, doth sleep;
  Or some great thought doth keep
Back the intelligence, and falsely swears
  They are base and idle fears
Whereof the loyal conscience so complains.
  Thus, by these subtle trains,
Do several passions invade the mind,
  And strike our reason blind,
Of which usurping rank, some have thought love
  The first; as prone to move
Most frequent tumults, horrors, and unrests
  In our enflamed breasts:
But this doth from the cloud of error grow,

Which thus we over-blow.
The thing they here call Love, is blind Desire,
   Armed with bow, shafts, and fire;
Inconstant, like the sea, of whence 'tis born,
   Rough, swelling, like a storm:
With whom who sails, rides on the surge of fear,
   And boils, as if he were
In a continual tempest. Now, true Love
   No such effects doth prove;
That is an essence far more gentle, fine,
   Pure, perfect, nay divine;
It is a golden chain let down from heaven,
   Whose links are bright and even,
That falls like sleep on lovers, and combines
   The soft, and sweetest minds
In equal knots: this bears no brands nor darts,
   To murther different hearts,
But in a calm and god-like unity
   Preserves community.
O, who is he that in this peace enjoys
   The Elixir of all joys?
A form more fresh than are the Eden bowers,
   And lasting as her flowers:
Richer than Time, and as Time's virtue rare:
   Sober, as saddest care;
A fixed thought, an eye untaught to glance:
   Who, blest with such high chance,
Would, at suggestion of a steep desire,
   Cast himself from the spire
Of all his happiness? But soft, I hear
   Some vicious fool draw near,
That cries we dream, and swears there's no such
      thing
   As this chaste love we sing.
Peace, Luxury, thou art like one of those
   Who, being at sea, suppose,

Because they move, the continent doth so.
   No, Vice, we let thee know,
Though thy wild thoughts with sparrows' wings do fly.
   Turtles can chastly die;
And yet (in this t' express ourselves more clear)
   We do not number here
Such spirits as are only continent,
   Because lust's means are spent:
Or those who doubt the common mouth of fame,
   And for their place and name,
Cannot so safely sin: their chastity
   Is mere necessity.
Nor mean we those whom vows and conscience
   Have filled with abstinence:
Though we acknowledge, who can so abstain,
   Makes a most blessed gain.
He that for love of goodness hateth ill,
   Is more crown-worthy still,
Than he which for sin's penalty forbears;
   His heart sins, though he fears.
But we propose a person like our Dove,
   Graced with a Phoenix' love;
A beauty of that clear and sparkling light,
   Would make a day of night,
And turn the blackest sorrows to bright joys;
   Whose odorous breath destroys
All taste of bitterness, and makes the air
   As sweet as she is fair.
A body so harmoniously composed,
   As if Nature disclosed
All her best symmetry in that one feature!
   O, so divine a creature,
Who could be false to? chiefly when he knows
   How only she bestows
The wealthy treasure of her love on him;

Making his fortunes swim
In the full flood of her admired perfection?
　What savage, brute affection,
Would not be fearful to offend a dame
　Of this excelling frame?
Much more a noble and right generous mind,
　To virtuous moods inclined,
That knows the weight of guilt; he will refrain
　From thoughts of such a strain,
And to his sense object this sentence ever,
　'Man may securely sin, but safely never.'

BEN JONSON

MARRIAGE

A Ballad upon a Wedding

I tell thee Dick where I have been,
Where I the rarest things have seen;
    O things without compare!
Such sights again cannot be found
In any place on English ground,
    Be it at Wake, or Fair.

At Charing Cross, hard by the way
Where we (thou knowest) do sell our hay,
    There is a house with stairs;
And there did I see coming down
Such folk as are not in our town,
    Forty at least, in Pairs.

Amongst the rest, one pestilent fine,
(His beard no bigger though than mine)
    Walked on before the rest:
Our Landlord looks like nothing to him:
The King (God bless him) 'twould undo him,
    Should he go still so dressed.

At Course-a-Park, without all doubt,
He should have just been taken out
    By all the maids i' the town:
Though lusty Roger there had been,
Or little George upon the Green,
    Or Vincent of the Crown.

But wot you what? the youth was going
To make an end for all his wooing;
    The parson for him stayed;
Yet by his leave, for all his haste,
He did not so much wish all past,
    Perchance, as did the maid.

The maid (and thereby hangs a tale)
For such a maid no Whitsun ale
   Could ever yet produce:
No grape that's kindly ripe, could be
So sound, so plump, so soft as she,
   Nor half so full of juice.

Her finger was so small, the ring
Would not stay on, which they did bring,
   It was too wide a peck;
And to say truth, for out it must,
It looked like a great collar, just
   About our young colt's neck.

Her feet beneath her petticoat,
Like little mice stole in and out,
   As if they feared the light:
But O she dances such a way
No sun upon an Easter day
   Is half so fine a sight.

He would have kissed her once or twice,
But she would not, she was so nice,
   She would not do't in sight,
And then she looked as who should say
I will do what I list today;
   And you shall do't at night.

Her cheeks so rare a white was on,
No daisy makes comparison,
   Who sees them is undone,
For streaks of red were mingled there,
Such as are on a Catherine pear,
   The side that's next to the sun.

Her lip's were red, and one was thin,
Compared to that was near her chin,
  (Some bee had stung it newly).
But, Dick, her eyes so guard her face,
I durst no more upon them gaze,
  Than on the sun in July.

Her mouth so small when she does speak,
Thou'dst swear her teeth her words did break,
  That they might passage get,
But she so handled still the matter,
They came as good as ours, or better,
  And are not spent a whit.

If wishing should be any sin,
The parson himself had guilty been,
  She looked that day so purely;
And did the youth so oft the feat
At night, as some did in conceit,
  It would have spoiled him, surely.

Just in the nick the cook knocked thrice,
And all the waiters in a trice
  His summons did obey,
Each serving man with dish in hand,
Marched boldly up, like our Trained Band,
  Presented, and away.

When all the meat was on the table,
What man of knife, or teeth, was able
  To stay to be entreated?
And this the very reason was,
Before the parson could say Grace,
  The company was seated.

111

The business of the kitchen's great,
For it is fit that men should eat;
   Nor was it there denied:
Passion o' me! How I run on!
There's that that would be thought upon,
   I trow, besides the bride.

Now hats fly off, and youths carouse;
Healths first go round, and then the house,
   The bride's came thick and thick;
And when 'twas named another's health,
Perhaps he made it hers by stealth.
   And who could help it, Dick?

O' the sudden up they rise and dance;
Then sit again, and sigh, and glance:
   Then dance again and kiss:
Thus several ways the time did pass,
Till every woman wished her place,
   And every man wished his.

By this time all were stol'n aside
To counsel and undress the bride;
   But that he must not know;
But yet 'twas thought he guessed her mind,
And did not mean to stay behind
   Above an hour or so.

When in he came, Dick, there she lay
Like new-fall'n snow melting away
   ('Twas time I trow to part);
Kisses were now the only stay,
Which soon she gave, as who would say,
   Good Boy! with all my heart.

But just as heavens would have to cross it,
In came the bridesmaids with the posset;
  The bridegroom eat in spite;
For he had left the women to't
It would have cost two hours to do't,
  Which were too much that night.

At length the candles out and out,
All that they had not done, they do't:
  What that is, who can tell?
But I believe it was no more
Than thou and I have done before
  With Briget, and with Nell.

SIR JOHN SUCKLING

Bridal Song

Hold back thy hours, old Night, till we have done;
  The day will come too soon;
Young maids will curse thee, if thou steal'st away
And leav'st their losses open to the day:
    Stay, stay, and hide
    The blushes of the bride.

Stay, gentle Night, and with thy darkness cover
  The kisses of her lover;
Stay, and confound her tears and her loud cryings,
Her weak denials, vows, and often-dyings;
    Stay, and hide all:
    But help not, though she call.

FRANCIS BEAUMONT

Hymen

Hymen, god of marriage-bed,
Be thou ever honourëd:
Thou, whose torch's purer light
Death's sad tapers did affright,
And instead of funeral fires
Kindled lovers' chaste desires:
    May their love
    Ever prove
True and constant; let not age
Know their youthful heat to assuage.

Maids, prepare the genial bed:
Then come, night, and hide that red
Which her cheeks, his heart does burn,
Till the envious day return,
And the lusty bridegroom say,
'I have chased her fears away,
    And instead
    Of virginhead,
Given her a greater good,
Perfection and womanhood.'

JOSEPH RUTTER

The Progress of Marriage

Aetatis suae fifty-two
A rich divine began to woo
A handsome young imperious girl
Nearly related to an Earl.
Her parents and her friends consent,
The couple to the temple went:
They first invite the Cyprian queen,
'Twas answered, she would not be seen.
The Graces next, and all the Muses
Were bid in form, but sent excuses:
Juno attended at the porch
With farthing candle for a torch,
While Mistress Iris held her train,
The faded bow distilling rain.
Then Hebe came and took her place
But showed no more than half her face.

Whate'er these dire forebodings meant,
In mirth the wedding-day was spent.
The wedding-day, you take me right,
I promise nothing for the night:
The bridegroom dressed, to make a figure,
Assumes an artificial vigour;
A flourished nightcap on, to grace
His ruddy, wrinkled, smirking face,
Like the faint red upon a pippin
Half withered by a winter's keeping.

And, thus set out this happy pair,
The swain is rich, the nymph is fair;
But, which I gladly would forget,
The swain is old, the nymph coquette.
Both from the goal together start;
Scarce run a step before they part;
No common ligament that binds

The various textures of their minds,
Their thoughts, and actions, hopes, and fears,
Less corresponding than their years.
Her spouse desires his coffee soon,
She rises to her tea at noon.
While he goes out to cheapen books,
She at the glass consults her looks;
While Betty's buzzing at her ear,
Lord, what a dress these parsons wear,
So odd a choice, how could she make,
Wished him a colonel for her sake.
Then on her fingers' ends she counts
Exact to what his age amounts,
The Dean, she heard her uncle say,
Is sixty, if he be a day;
His ruddy cheeks are no disguise;
You see the crow's feet round his eyes.

   At one she rambles to the shops
To cheapen tea, and talk with fops.
Or calls a council of her maids
And tradesmen, to compare brocades.
Her weighty morning business o'er
Sits down to dinner just at four;
Minds nothing that is done or said,
Her evening work so fills her head;
The Dean, who used to dine at one,
Is mawkish, and his stomach gone;
In threadbare gown, would scarce a louse hold,
Looks like the chaplain of the household,
Beholds her from the chaplain's place
In French brocades and Flanders lace;
He wonders what employs her brain;
But never asks, or asks in vain;
His mind is full of other cares,

And in the sneaking parson's airs
Computes, that half a parish dues
Will hardly find his wife in shoes.

Canst thou imagine, dull divine,
'Twill gain her love to make her fine?
Hath she no other wants beside?
You raise desire as well as pride,
Enticing coxcombs to adore,
And teach her to despise thee more.

If in her coach she'll condescend
To place him at the hinder end
Her hoop is hoist above his nose,
His odious gown would soil her clothes,
And drops him at the church, to pray
While she drives on to see the play.
He like an orderly divine
Comes home a quarter after nine,
And meets her hasting to the ball,
Her chairmen push him from the wall:
He enters in, and walks upstairs,
And calls the family to prayers,
Then goes alone to take his rest
In bed, where he can spare her best.
At five the footmen make a din,
Her ladyship is just come in,
The masquerade began at two,
She stole away with much ado,
And shall be chid this afternoon
For leaving company so soon;
She'll say, and she may truly say't,
She can't abide to stay out late.

But now, though scarce a twelve month
   married,
His lady has twelve times miscarried,
The cause, alas, is quickly guessed,

118

Marriage

The town has whispered round the jest:
Think on some remedy in time,
You find his Reverence past his prime,
Already dwindled to a lathe;
No other way but try the Bath.

For Venus rising from the ocean
Infused a strong prolific potion,
That mixed with Achelous' spring,
The 'hornéd flood', as poets sing:
Who with an English beauty smitten
Ran underground from Greece to Britain,
The genial virtue with him brought,
And gave the nymph a plenteous draught;
Then fled, and left his horn behind
For husbands past their youth to find;
The nymph who still with passion burned,
Was to a boiling fountain turned,
Where childless wives crowd every morn
To drink in Achelous' horn.
And here the father often gains
That title by another's pains.

Hither, though much against his grain,
The Dean has carried Lady Jane.
He for a while would not consent,
But vowed his money all was spent;
His money spent! a clownish reason!
And must my Lady slip her season?
The doctor with a double fee
Was bribed to make the Dean agree.

Here, all diversions of the place
Are proper in my Lady's case:
With which she patiently complies,
Merely because her friends advise;

His money and her time employs
In music, raffling-rooms, and toys,
Or in the Cross Bath, seeks an heir
Since others oft have found one there;
Where if the Dean by chance appears
It shames his cassock and his years.
He keeps his distance in the gallery
Till banished by some coxcomb's raillery;
For, it would his character expose
To bathe among the belles and beaux.

So have I seen within a pen
Young ducklings, fostered by a hen;
But when let out, they run and muddle
As instinct leads them, in a puddle;
The sober hen not born to swim
With mournful note clucks round the brim.

The Dean with all his best endeavour
Gets not an heir, but gets a fever;
A victim to the last essays
Of vigour in declining days.
He dies, and leaves his mourning mate
(What could he less?) his whole estate.

The widow goes through all the forms;
New lovers now will come in swarms.
Oh, may I see her soon dispensing
Her favours to some broken ensign!
Him let her marry for his face,
And only coat of tarnished lace;
To turn her naked out of doors,
And spend her jointure on his whores:
But for a parting present leave her
A rooted pox to last forever.

JONATHAN SWIFT

Epithalamion Made at Lincoln's Inn

The sun-beams in the east are spread,
Leave, leave, fair Bride, your solitary bed,
   No more shall you return to it alone,
It nurseth sadness, and your body's print,
Like to a grave, the yielding down doth dint;
    You and your other you meet there anon;
      Put forth, put forth that warm balm-breathing thigh.
Which when next time you in these sheets will smother
There it must meet another,
      Which never was, but must be, oft, more nigh;
Come glad from thence, go gladder than you came,
Today put on perfection, and a woman's name.

Daughters of London, you which be
Our golden mines, and furnished treasury,
   You which are angels, yet still bring with you
Thousands of angels on your marriage days,
Help with your presence, and device, to praise
    These rites, which also unto you grow due;
      Conceitedly dress her, and be assigned,
By you, fit place for every flower and jewel,
Make her for love fit fuel
     As gay as Flora, and as rich as Ind;
So may she fair and rich, in nothing lame,
Today put on perfection, and a woman's name.

And you frolic patricians,
Sons of these senators' wealth's deep oceans,
   Ye painted courtiers, barrels of others' wits,
Ye country men, who but your beasts love none,
Ye of those fellowships whereof he's one,
    Of study and play made strange hermaphrodites,
      Here shine; this Bridegroom to the Temple bring.
Lo, in yon path which store of strewed flowers graceth,
The sober virgin paceth;

Except my sight fail, 'tis no other thing;
Weep not nor blush, here is no grief nor shame,
Today put on perfection, and a woman's name.

Thy two-leaved gates fair Temple unfold,
And these two in thy sacred bosom hold,
    Till, mystically joined, but one they be;
Then may thy lean and hunger-starved womb
Long time expect their bodies and their tomb,
    Long after their own parents fatten thee.
All elder claims, and all cold barrenness,
All yielding to new loves be far for ever,
Which might these two dissever,
    Always, all th'other may each one possess;
For, the best Bride, best worthy of praise and fame,
Today puts on perfection, and a woman's name.

Oh winter days bring much delight,
Not for themselves, but for they soon bring night;
    Other sweets wait thee than these diverse meats,
Other disports than dancing jollities,
Other love tricks than glancing with the eyes,
    But that the sun still in our half sphere sweats;
    He flies in winter, but he now stands still,
Yet shadows turn; noon point he hath attained,
His steeds nill be restrained,
    But gallop lively down the western hill;
Thou shalt, when he hath run the world's half frame,
Tonight put on perfection, and a woman's name.

The amorous evening star is rose,
Why then should not our amorous star inclose
    Herself in her wished bed? Release your strings
Musicians, and dancers take some truce
With these your pleasing labours, for great use

Marriage

As much weariness as perfection brings;
   You, and not only you, but all toiled beasts
Rest duly; at night all their toils are dispensed;
But in their beds commenced
   Are other labours, and more dainty feasts;
She goes a maid, who, lest she turn the same,
Tonight puts on perfection, and a woman's name.

Thy virgin's girdle now untie,
   And in thy nuptial bed (love's altar) lie
   A pleasing sacrifice; now dispossess
Thee of these chains and robes which were put on
T' adorn the day, not thee; for thou, alone,
   Like virtue and truth, art best in nakedness;
     This bed is only to virginity
A grave, but, to a better state, a cradle;
Till now thou wast but able
   To be what now thou art; then that by thee
No more be said, *I may be,* but, *I am,*
Tonight put on perfection, and a woman's name.

Even like a faithful man content,
   That this life for a better should be spent:
   So, she a mother's rich style doth prefer,
And at the Bridegroom's wished approach doth lie,
Like an appointed lamb, when tenderly
   The priest comes on his knees t' embowel her;
     Now sleep or watch with more joy; and O light
Of heaven, to morrow rise thou hot, and early;
This sun will love so dearly
   Her rest, that long, long we shall want her sight;
Wonders are wrought, for she which had no maim,
Tonight puts on perfection, and a woman's name.

JOHN DONNE

The Flea

Mark but this flea, and mark in this,
How little that which thou deny'st me is;
Me it sucked first, and now sucks thee,
And in this flea, our two bloods mingled be;
Confess it, this cannot be said
A sin, or shame, or loss of maidenhead,
   Yet this enjoys before it woo,
     And pampered swells with one blood made of
      two,
     And this, alas, is more than we would do.

Oh stay, three lives in one flea spare,
Where we almost, nay more than married are.
This flea is you and I, and this
Our marriage bed, and marriage temple is;
Though parents grudge, and you, we'are met,
And cloistered in these living walls of jet.
   Though use make you apt to kill me,
   Let not to this, self murder added be,
   And sacrilege, three sins in killing three.

Cruel and sudden, hast thou since
Purpled thy nail, in blood of innocence?
In what could this flea guilty be,
Except in that drop which it sucked from thee?
Yet thou triumph'st, and say'st that thou
Find'st not thyself, nor me the weaker now;
   'Tis true, then learn how false, fears be;
   Just so much honour, when thou yield'st to me,
   Will waste, as this flea's death took life from thee.

JOHN DONNE

For My Lover,
Returning to His Wife

She is all there.
She was melted carefully down for you
and cast up from your childhood,
cast up from your one hundred favorite aggies.

She has always been there, my darling.
She is, in fact, exquisite.
Fireworks in the dull middle of February
and as real as a cast-iron pot.

Let's face it, I have been momentary.
A luxury. A bright red sloop in the harbor.
My hair rising like smoke from the car window.
Littleneck clams out of season.

She is more than that. She is your have to have,
has grown you your practical your tropical growth.
This is not an experiment. She is all harmony.
She sees to oars and oarlocks for the dinghy,

has placed wild flowers at the window at breakfast,
sat by the potter's wheel at midday,
set forth three children under the moon,
three cherubs drawn by Michelangelo,

done this with her legs spread out
in the terrible months in the chapel.
If you glance up, the children are there
like delicate balloons resting on the ceiling.

She has also carried each one down the hall
after supper, their heads privately bent,
two legs protesting, person to person,

her face flushed with a song and their little sleep.

I give you back your heart.
I give you permission —

for the fuse inside her, throbbing
angrily in the dirt, for the bitch in her
and the burying of her wound —
for the burying of her small red wound alive —

for the pale flickering flare under her ribs,
for the drunken sailor who waits in her left pulse,
for the mother's knee, for the stockings,
for the garter belt, for the call —

the curious call
when you will burrow in arms and breasts
and tug at the orange ribbon in her hair
and answer the call, the curious call.

She is so naked and singular.
She is the sum of yourself and your dream.
Climb her like a monument, step after step.
She is solid.

As for me, I am a watercolor.
I wash off.

ANNE SEXTON

DREAMS

The Vine

I dream'd this mortal part of mine
Was Metamorphos'd to a Vine;
Which crawling one and every way,
Enthrall'd my dainty Lucia.
Me thought, her long small legs and thighs
I with my Tendrils did surprise;
Her Belly, Buttocks, and her Waist
By my soft Nerv'lets were embrac'd:
About her head I writhing hung,
And with rich clusters (hid among
The leaves) her temples I behung:
So that my Lucia seem'd to me
Young Bacchus ravisht by his tree.
My curls about her neck did crawl,
And arms and hands they did enthral:
So that she could not freely stir,
(All parts there made one prisoner.)
But when I crept with leaves to hide
Those parts, which maids keep unespy'd,
Such fleeting pleasures there I took,
That with the fancy I awoke;
And found (Ah me!) this flesh of mine
More like a Stock, than like a Vine.

ROBERT HERRICK

A Dream Broke

As Nilus sudden Ebbing, here
Doth leave a scale, and a scale there,
And somewhere else perhaps a Fin,
Which by his stay had Fishes been:
So Dreams, which overflowing be,
Departing leave Half-things, which we
For their Imperfectness can call
But Joys i'th' Fin, or in the Scale.
If when her Tears I haste to kiss,
They dry up, and deceive my Bliss,
May not I say the Waters sink,
And cheat my Thirst when I would drink?
If when her Breasts I go to press,
Instead of them I grasp her Dress,
May not I say the Apples then
Are set down, and snatch'd up again?
Sleep was not thus Death's Brother meant;
'Twas made an Ease, no Punishment.
As then that's finish'd by the Sun,
Which Nile did only leave begun,
My Fancy shall run o'r Sleeps Themes,
And so make up the Web of Dreams:
In vain sweet shades, ye do Contest:
Awak'd how e'r I'll think the rest.

WILLIAM CARTWRIGHT

The Vision to Electra

I dream'd we both were in a bed
Of Roses, almost smothered:
The warmth and sweetness had me there
Made lovingly familiar:
But that I heard thy sweet breath say,
Faults done by night, will blush by day:
I kist thee (panting,) and I call
Night to the Record! that was all.
But ah! if empty dreams so please,
Love give me more such nights as these.

ROBERT HERRICK

The Man Under the Bed

The man under the bed
The man who has been there for years waiting
The man who waits for my floating bare foot
The man who is silent as dustballs riding the darkness
The man whose breath is the breathing of small white
    butterflies
The man whose breathing I hear when I pick up the
    phone
The man in the mirror whose breath blackens silver
The boneman in closets who rattles the mothballs
The man at the end of the end of the line

I met him tonight   I always meet him
He stands in the amber air of a bar
When the shrimp curl like beckoning fingers
& ride through the air on their toothpick skewers
When the ice cracks & I am about to fall through
he arranges his face around its hollows
he opens his pupilless eyes at me
For years he has waited to drag me down
& now he tells me
he has only waited to take me home
We waltz through the street like death & the maiden
We float through the wall of the wall of my room

If he's my dream he will fold back into my body
His breath writes letters of mist on the glass of my cheeks
I wrap myself around him like the darkness
I breathe into his mouth
& make him real

ERICA JONG

132

DILEMMAS

Oh, blush not so, oh, blush not so

Oh, blush not so, oh, blush not so,
    Or I shall think ye knowing.
And if ye smile the blushing while,
    Then maidenheads are going.

There's a blush for won't, and a blush for shan't —
    And a blush for having done it.
There's a blush for thought, and a blush for naught,
    And a blush for just begun it.

Oh, sigh not so, oh, sigh not so,
    For it sounds of Eve's sweet pippin.
By those loosened hips you have tasted the pips
    And fought in an amorous nipping.

Will you play once more at nice-cut-core,
    For it only will last our youth out?
And we have the prime of the kissing time,
    We have not one sweet tooth out.

There's a sigh for yes, and a sigh for no,
    And a sigh for I can't bear it!
Oh, what can be done, shall we stay or run?
    Oh, cut the sweet apple and share it!

JOHN KEATS

Ode

Was ever man of Nature's framing
  So given o'er to roving,
Who have been twenty years a taming
By ways that are not worth the naming,
  And now must die of loving?

Hell take me if she been't so winning
  That now I love her mainly,
And though in jest at the beginning,
Yet now I'd wond'rous fain be sinning,
  And so have told her plainly.

At which she cries I do not love her,
  And tells me of her Honour;
Then have I no way to disprove her,
And my true passion to discover,
  But straight to fall upon her.

Which done, forsooth, she talks of wedding,
  But what will that avail her?
For though I am old Dog at Bedding,
I'm yet a man of so much reading,
  That there I sure shall fail her.

No, hang me if I ever marry,
  Till Womankind grow stauncher:
I do delight delights to vary,
And love not in one Hulk to tarry,
  But only Trim and Launch her.

CHARLES COTTON

Down in a Garden

Down in a garden sat my dearest Love,
Her skin more soft and white than down of swan,
More tender-hearted than the turtle-dove,
And far more kind than bleeding pelican.
I courted her; she rose and blushing said,
'Why was I born to live and die a maid?'
With that I plucked a pretty marigold,
Whose dewy leaves shut up when day is done:
'Sweeting,' I said, 'arise, look and behold,
A pretty riddle I'll to thee unfold:
These leaves shut in as close as cloistered nun,
Yet will they open when they see the sun.'
'What mean you by this riddle, sir?' she said,
'I pray expound it.' Then I thus began:
'Know maids are made for men, man for a maid.'
With that she changed her colour and grew wan:
'Since that this riddle you so well unfold,
Be you the sun, I'll be the marigold.'

ANON

When Man Enters Woman

When man
enters woman,
like the surf biting the shore,
again and again,
and the woman opens her mouth in
    pleasure
and her teeth gleam
like the alphabet,
Logos appears milking a star,
and the man
inside of woman
ties a knot
so that they will
never again be separate
and the woman
climbs into a flower
and swallows its stem
and Logos appears
and unleashes their rivers.

This man,
this woman
with their double hunger,
have tried to reach through
the curtain of God
and briefly they have,
though God
in His perversity
unties the knot.

ANNE SEXTON

They flee from me

They flee from me that sometime did me seek
With naked foot stalking in my chamber.
I have seen them gentle, tame and meek
    That now are wild and do not remember
    That sometime they put themself in danger
To take bread at my hand; and now they range
Busily seeking with a continual change.

Thankèd be fortune it hath been otherwise
    Twenty times better: but once in special,
In thin array after a pleasant guise,
    When her loose gown from her shoulders did fall,
    And she me caught in her arms long and small;
Therewithal sweetly did me kiss,
And softly said, 'Dear heart, how like you this?'

It was no dream: I lay broad waking.
    But all is turned through my gentleness
Into a strange fashion of forsaking;
    And I have leave to go of her goodness,
    And she also to use new-fangledness.
But since that I so kindly am served,
I would fain know what she hath deserved.

SIR THOMAS WYATT

To a Lady to Answer Directly
with Yea or Nay

Madam, withouten many words,
   Once, I am sure, ye will or no:
And if ye will, then leave your bords
   And use your wit and show it so:
And with a beck ye shall me call;
   And if of one, that burneth alway,
Ye have any pity at all,
   Answer him fair with yea, or nay.
If it be yea, I shall be fain;
   If it be nay, friends as before;
Ye shall another man obtain,
   And I mine own and yours no more.

SIR THOMAS WYATT

bords: jokes, games

A Lover's Anger

As Chloe came into the room t'other day,
I peevish began, 'Where so long could you stay?
In your life-time you never regarded your hour:
You promised at two; and (pray look, child) 'tis four.
A lady's watch needs neither figures nor wheels:
'Tis enough, that 'tis loaded with baubles and seals.
A temper so heedless no mortal can bear — '
Thus far I went on with a resolute air.
'Lord bless me!' said she; 'let a body but speak:
Here's an ugly hard rose-bud fall'n into my neck;
It has hurt me and vexed me to such a degree —
See here! for you never believe me; pray see,
On the left side my breast what a mark it has made!'
So saying, her bosom she careless displayed.
That seat of delight I with wonder surveyed,
And forgot every word I designed to have said.

MATTHEW PRIOR

Nine Inch Will Please a Lady

1

'Come rede me, dame, come tell me, dame,
  'My dame come tell me truly,
'What length o' graith, when weel ca'd hame,
  'Will sair a woman duly?'
The carlin clew her wanton tail,
  Her wanton tail sae ready —
I learn'd a sang in Annandale,
  Nine inch will please a lady. —

2

But for a koontrie c — nt like mine,
  In sooth, we're nae sae gentle;
We'll tak tway thumb-bread to the nine,
  And that's a sonsy p — ntle:
O Leeze me on my Charlie lad,
  I'll ne'er forget my Charlie!
Tway roarin handfu's and a daud,
  He nidge't it in fu' rarely. —

3

But weary fa' the laithron doup,
  And may it ne'er be thrivin!
It's no the length that maks me loup,
  But it's the double drivin. —
Come nidge me, Tam, come nudge me, Tam,
  Come nidge me o'er the nyvel!
Come lowse and lug your battering ram,
  And thrash him at my gyvel!

ANON/ROBERT BURNS

O Leeze me on: give me great pleasure

Ode to Spring

When maukin bucks, at early f — s,
    In dewy grass are seen, Sir;
And birds, on boughs, take off their m — s,
    Amang the leaves sae green, Sir;
Latona's son looks liquorish on
    Dame Nature's grand impètus,
Till his p — go rise, then westward flies
    To r — ger Madame Thetis.

Yon wandering rill that marks the hill,
    And glances o'er the brae, Sir,
Glides by a bower where many a flower
    Sheds fragrance on the day, Sir;

There Damon lay, with Sylvia gay,
    To love they thought no crime, Sir;
The wild-birds sang, the echoes rang,
    While Damon's a — se beat time, Sir. —

First, wi' the thrush, his thrust and push
    Had compass large and long, Sir;
The blackbird next, his tuneful text,
    Was bolder, clear and strong, Sir;
The linnet's lay came then in play,
    And the lark that soar'd aboon, Sir;
Till Damon, fierce, mistim'd his a — ,
    And f — 'd quite out of tune, Sir. —

ROBERT BURNS

143

Upon His Leaving His Mistress

'Tis not that I am weary grown
Of being yours, and yours alone;
But with what face can I incline
To damn you to be only mine?
   You, whom some kinder power did fashion,
   By merit and by inclination,
   The joy at least of one whole nation.

Let meaner spirits of your sex
With humbler aims their thoughts perplex,
And boast if by their arts they can
Contrive to make *one* happy man;
   Whilst, moved by an impartial sense,
   Favours like nature you dispense
   With universal influence.

See, the kind seed-receiving earth
To every grain affords a birth.
On her no showers unwelcome fall;
Her willing womb retains 'em all.
   And shall my Celia be confined?
   No! Live up to thy mighty mind,
   And be the mistress of mankind.

JOHN WILMOT, EARL OF ROCHESTER

The Fall

How blest was the created state
  Of man and woman, ere they fell,
Compared to our unhappy fate:
  We need not fear another hell.

Naked beneath cool shades they lay;
  Enjoyment waited on desire;
Each member did their wills obey,
  Nor could a wish set pleasure higher.

But we, poor slaves to hope and fear,
  Are never of our joys secure;
They lessen still as they draw near,
  And none but dull delights endure.

Then, Chloris, while I duly pay
  The nobler tribute of my heart,
Be not you so severe to say
  You love me for the frailer part.

JOHN WILMOT, EARL OF ROCHESTER

From Bed to Verse

Her Man Described by her own Dictamen

Of your trouble, Ben, to ease me,
I will tell what Man would please me.
I would have him, if I could,
Noble; or of greater blood;
Titles, I confess, do take me,
And a woman God did make me;
French to boot, at least in fashion,
And his manners of that nation.

Young I'd have him too, and fair,
Yet a man; with crisped hair,
Cast in thousand snares and rings,
For Love's fingers, and his wings:
Chestnut colour, or more slack,
Gold, upon a ground of black.
Venus and Minerva's eyes,
For he must look wanton-wise.

Eyebrows bent like Cupid's bow,
Front, an ample field of snow;
Even nose, and cheek withal,
Smooth as is the billiard-ball:
Chin as woolly as the peach;
And his lip should kissing teach,
Till he cherished too much beard,
And made Love or me afeard.

He should have a hand as soft
As the down, and show it oft;
Skin as smooth as any rush,
And so thin to see a blush
Rising through it ere it came;
All his blood should be a flame,
Quickly fired, as in beginners
In Love's school, and yet no sinners.
'Twere too long to speak of all:

What we harmony do call
In a body should be there.
Well he should his clothes, too, wear,
Yet no tailor help to make him;
Drest, you still for man should take him,
And not think h' had eat a stake,
Or were set up in a brake.
  Valiant he should be as fire,
Showing danger more than ire.
Bounteous as the clouds to earth,
And as honest as his birth;
All his actions to be such,
As to do no thing too much:
Nor o'er-praise, nor yet condemn,
Nor out-value, nor contemn;
Nor do wrongs, nor wrongs receive,
Nor tie knots, nor knots unweave;
And from baseness to be free,
As he durst love Truth and me.
  Such a man, with every part,
I could give my very heart;
But of one if short he came,
I can rest me where I am.

BEN JONSON

Where It Begins

The corruption begins with the eyes,
the page, the hunger.
It hangs on the first hook
of the first comma.

The mouth shuts & opens.
Newspapers are there & nursery rhymes.
Readers, lovers dangle
like Cassius, Brutus
from Satan's teeth.

The corruption begins with the mouth,
the tongue, the wanting.
The first poem in the world
is *I want to eat.*

The breast is the screen
of the dream;
no hungry poet
can ever be content
with two.

The corruption begins with the breasts,
the cunt, the navel.
It begins with wanting love
from strangers.

The breasts are two blind animals
with painted eyes.
The cunt is a furry deaf mute
speaking a red tongue.
The tongue is hunger.

The corruption begins with the curled snail
of the baby.

It begins with the white flood
of love on pages.

It begins with emptiness
where love begins.
It begins with love
where emptiness
begins.

ERICA JONG

OUTRAGE AND REMORSE

Mr Etherege's Answer to a Letter from Lord Buckhurst

So soft and amorously you write
Of cunt and prick, the cunt's delight,
That were I still in lantern sweating,
Swallowing of bolus or a-spitting,
I should forgive each injury
The pocky whores have offered me,
And only of my fate complain
Because I must from cunt abstain.
The powerful cunt! whose very name
Kindles in me an amorous flame!
Begins to make my pintle rise,
And long again to fight Love's prize!
Forgetful of those many scars
Which he has gotten in those wars.
This shows Love's chiefest magic lies
In women's cunts, not in their eyes:
There Cupid does his revels keep,
There lovers all their sorrows steep;
For having once but tasted that,
Their mysteries are quite forgot.
This may suffice to let you know
That I to cunt am not a foe,
Though you are pleased to think me so;
'Tis strange his zeal should be in suspicion
Who dies a martyr for's religion.
   But now to give you an account
Of Cuffley, that whore paramount!
Cuffley! whose beauty warms the age,
And fills our youth with love and rage,
Who like fierce wolves pursue the game,
While secretly the lecherous dame
With some choice gallant takes her flight

bolus: supposed cure for the pox

153

And in a corner fucks all night.
Then the next morning we all hunt
To find whose fingers smell of cunt,
With jealousy and envy moved
Against the man that was beloved.
Whilst you to Echo teach her name,
Thus it becomes the voice of fame
In every corner of the Town.
We here proclaim her high renown
Whilst you within some neighbouring grove
Indite the story of your love,
And with your penknife keen and bright,
On stately trees your passion write,
So that each nymph that passes through
Must envy her and pity you.
We at the Fleece or at the Bear,
With good case knife, well whet on stair
(A gentle weapon, made to feed
Mankind and not to let him bleed)
A thousand amorous fancies scrape.
There's not a pewter dish can scape
Without her name or arms which are
The same that Love himself does bear.
  Here one, to show you love's no glutton,
In the midst of supper leaves his mutton,
And on his greasy plate, with care,
Carves the bright image of the fair.
  Another, though a drunken sot,
Neglects his wine and on the pot
A band of naked Cupids draws,
With pricks no bigger than wheat straws.
Then on a nasty candlestick
One figures Love's hieroglyphic,
A couchant cunt and rampant prick.
And that the sight may more inflame,

The lookers-on subscribe her name:
Cuffley! — her sex's pride and shame.
There's not a man but does discover
By some such action he's her lover.
  But now 'tis time to give her over,
And let your Lordship know you are
The mistress that employs our care.
Your absence makes us melancholy,
Nor drink nor cunt can make us jolly,
Unless we've you within our arms,
In whom there dwells diviner charms.
Then quit with speed your pensive grove
And here in Town pursue your love;
Where at your coming you shall find
Your servants glad, your mistress kind,
All things devoted to your mind.

GEORGE ETHEREGE

No, no, fair heretic

No, no, fair heretic, it needs must be
　　But an ill love in me,
　　And worse for thee;
For were it in my power,
To love thee now this hour
　　More than I did the last;
I would then so fall
　　I might not love at all;
Love that can flow, and can admit increase,
Admits as well an ebb, and may grow less.

True love is still the same; the Torrid Zones,
　　And those more frigid ones
　　It must not know:
For love grown cold or hot,
　　Is lust or friendship, not
　　The thing we have.
For that's a flame would die
　　Held down, or up too high:
Then think I love more than I can express,
And would love more could I but love thee less.

SIR JOHN SUCKLING

156

Two loves I have, of comfort and despair

Two loves I have, of comfort and despair,
Which like two spirits do suggest me still.
The better angel is a man right fair,
The worser spirit a woman colour'd ill.
To win me soon to hell, my female evil
Tempteth my better angel from my side,
And would corrupt my saint to be a devil,
Wooing his purity with her foul pride.
And whether that my angel be turn'd fiend
Suspect I may, yet not directly tell;
But being both from me, both to each friend,
I guess one angel in another's hell.
    Yet this shall I ne'er know, but live in doubt,
    Till my bad angel fire my good one out.

WILLIAM SHAKESPEARE

Till my bad angel . . . : until my evil angel has infected my good
one with venereal disease

Upon T[om] C[arew?] Having the P[ox]

Troth, Tom, I must confess I much admire
Thy water should find passage through the fire;
For fire and water never could agree:
These now by nature have some sympathy.
Sure then his way he forces, for all know
The French ne'er grants a passage to his foe.
If it be so, his valour I must praise,
That being the weaker, yet can force his ways;
And wish that to his valour he had strength,
That he might drive the fire quite out at length;
For, troth, as yet the fire gets the day,
For evermore the water runs away.

SIR JOHN SUCKLING

fire: clap (or pox)

The Scar-fire

Water, water I desire,
Here's a house of flesh on fire:
Ope' the fountains and the springs,
And come all to Bucketings:
What ye cannot quench, pull down;
Spoil a house, to save a town:
Better tis that one shou'd fall,
Then by one, to hazard all.

ROBERT HERRICK

Human Relations

My mind is so evil and unjust
I smile in deprecation when I am flattered
But inside the palace of my smile
Is the grovelling worm that eats its own tail
And concealed under the threshold of my lips
Is the trustless word that will wrong you if it can.
Come nearer to me therefore, my friend,
And be impressed with the truth of my
    explanation.
No less, lady, take my chaste hand
While the other imaginatively rifles your drawers.

C. H. SISSON

All night by the rose

All night by the rose, rose —
    All night by the rose I lay;
Dared I not the rose steal,
    And yet I bore the flower away.

ANON

The Lover's Song

Bird sighs for the air,
Thought for I know not where,
For the womb the seed sighs.
Now sinks the same rest
On mind, on nest,
On straining thighs.

W. B. YEATS

The Spur

You think it horrible that lust and rage
Should dance attendance on my old age;
They were not such a plague when I was young;
What else have I to spur me into song?

W. B. YEATS

To Amarantha, That she would dishevel her hair

Amarantha sweet and fair,
Ah braid no more that shining hair!
  As my curious hand or eye,
Hovering round thee let it flie.

  Let it flie as unconfin'd
As its calm Ravisher, the wind;
  Who hath left his darling th'East,
To wanton o'er that spicy Nest.

  Ev'ry Tress must be confest
But neatly tangled at the best;
  Like a Clue of golden thread,
Most excellently ravelled.

  Do not then wind up that light
In Ribands, and o'er cloud in Night;
  Like the Sun in's early ray,
But shake your head and scatter day.

  See 'tis broke! Within this Grove
The Bower, and the walks of Love,
  Weary lie we down and rest,
And fan each other's panting breast.

  Here we'll strip and cool our fire
In Cream below, in milk-baths higher:
  And when all Wells are drawn dry,
I'll drink a tear out of thine eye.

  Which our very Joys shall leave
That sorrows thus we can deceive;
  Or our very sorrows weep,
That joys so ripe, so little keep.

RICHARD LOVELACE

from *Song of Myself*

Twenty-eight young men bathe by the shore,
Twenty-eight young men and all so friendly;
Twenty-eight years of womanly life and all so lonesome.

She owns the fine house by the rise of the bank,
She hides handsome and richly drest aft the blinds of the
    window.

Which of the young men does she like the best?
Ah the homeliest of them is beautiful to her.

Where are you off to, lady? for I see you,
You splash in the water there, yet stay stock still in your
    room.

Dancing and laughing along the beach came the twenty-
    ninth bather,
The rest did not see her, but she saw them and loved
    them.

The beards of the young men glisten'd with wet, it ran
    from their long hair,
Little streams pass'd all over their bodies.

An unseen hand also pass'd over their bodies,
It descended tremblingly from their temples and ribs.

The young men float on their backs, their white bellies
    bulge to the sun, they do not ask who seizes fast to
    them,
They do not know who puffs and declines with pendant
    and bending arch,
They do not think whom they souse with spray.

*   *   *

This is the meal equally set, this the meat for natural
    hunger,
It is for the wicked just the same as the righteous, I make
    appointments with all,
I will not have a single person slighted or left away,
The kept-woman, sponger, thief, are hereby invited,
The heavy-lipp'd slave is invited, the venerealee is
    invited;
There shall be no difference between them and the rest.

This is the press of a bashful hand, this the float and
    odor of hair,
This the touch of my lips to yours, this the murmur of
    yearning,
This the far-off depth and height reflecting my own face,
This the thoughtful merge of myself, and the outlet
    again.

Do you guess I have some intricate purpose?
Well I have, for the Fourth-month showers have, and the
    mica on the side of a rock has.

Do you take it I would astonish?
Does the daylight astonish? does the early redstart
    twittering through the woods?
Do I astonish more than they?

This hour I tell things in confidence,
I might not tell everybody, but I will tell you.

*   *   *

Walt Whitman, a kosmos, of Manhattan the son,
Turbulent, fleshy, sensual, eating, drinking and
    breeding,

No sentimentalist, no stander above men and women or
    apart from them,
No more modest than immodest.

Unscrew the locks from the doors!
Unscrew the doors themselves from their jambs!

Whoever degrades another degrades me,
And whatever is done or said returns at last to me.

Through me the afflatus surging and surging, through
    me the current and index.

I speak the pass-word primeval, I give the sign of
    democracy,
By God! I will accept nothing which all cannot have their
    counterpart of on the same terms.

Through me many long dumb voices,
Voices of the interminable generations of prisoners and
    slaves,
Voices of the diseas'd and despairing and of thieves and
    dwarfs,
Voices of cycles of preparation and accretion,
And of the threads that connect the stars, and of wombs
    and of the father-stuff,
And of the rights of them the others are down upon,
Of the deform'd, trivial, flat, foolish, despised,
Fog in the air, beetles rolling balls of dung.

Through me forbidden voices,
Voices of sexes and lusts, voices veil'd and I remove the
    veil,
Voices indecent by me clarified and transfigur'd.

I do not press my fingers across my mouth,
I keep as delicate around the bowels as around the head
and heart,
Copulation is no more rank to me than death is.

I believe in the flesh and the appetites,
Seeing, hearing, feeling, are miracles, and each part and
tag of me is a miracle.

Divine am I inside and out, and I make holy whatever I
touch or am touch'd from,
The scent of these arm-pits aroma finer than prayer,
This head more than churches, bibles, and all the creeds.

If I worship one thing more than another it shall be the
spread of my own body, or any part of it,
Translucent mould of me it shall be you!
Shaded ledges and rests it shall be you!
Firm masculine colter it shall be you!
Whatever goes to the tilth of me it shall be you!
You my rich blood! your milky stream pale strippings of
my life!
Breast that presses against other breasts it shall be you!
My brain it shall be your occult convolutions!
Root of wash'd sweet-flag! timorous pond-snipe! nest of
guarded duplicate eggs! it shall be you!
Mix'd tussled hay of head, beard, brawn, it shall be you!
Trickling sap of maple, fibre of manly wheat, it shall be
you!
Sun so generous it shall be you!
Vapors lighting and shading my face it shall be you!
You sweaty brooks and dews it shall be you!
Winds whose soft-tickling genitals rub against me it shall
be you!

Broad muscular fields, branches of live oak, loving
lounger in my winding paths, it shall be you!

Hands I have taken, face I have kiss'd, mortal I have ever
   touch'd, it shall be you.

I dote on myself, there is that lot of me and all so
      luscious,
Each moment and whatever happens thrills me with joy,
I cannot tell how my ankles bend, nor whence the cause
      of my faintest wish,
Nor the cause of the friendship I emit, nor the cause of
   the friendship I take again.

That I walk up my stoop, I pause to consider if it really
      be,
A morning-glory at my window satisfies me more than
   the metaphysics of books.

To behold the day-break!
The little light fades the immense and diaphanous
      shadows,
The air tastes good to my palate.

Hefts of the moving world at innocent gambols silently
      rising freshly exuding,
Scooting obliquely high and low.

Something I cannot see puts upward libidinous prongs,
Seas of bright juice suffuse heaven.

The earth by the sky staid with, the daily close of their
      junction,
The heav'd challenge from the east that moment over my
      head,
The mocking taunt, See then whether you shall be
      master!

WALT WHITMAN

Without Prejudice

To Spindle, Shears, and Rod,
Solicitors for God:
Dear madams, ref. the part
Enclosed herewith, my heart —
Please note this doesn't fit
The rest of the love kit
Supplied me by our father,
Your client, being rather
Too big to go with my head
Yet not big enough in bed.

ROBERT NYE

Fie, Pleasure, Fie!

Fie, pleasure, fie! thou cloyest me with delight;
   Thou fill'st my mouth with sweetmeats overmuch;
I wallow still in joy both day and night:
   I deem, I dream, I do, I taste, I touch
No thing but all that smells of perfect bliss,
Fie, pleasure, fie! I cannot like of this.

To taste, sometimes, a bait of bitter gall,
   To drink a draught of soür ale, some season,
To eat brown bread with homely hands in hall,
   Doth much increase men's appetites, by reason,
And makes the sweet more sugared that ensues,
Since minds of men do still seek after news.

It might suffice that Love hath built his bower
   Between my lady's lively shining eyes;
It were enough that beauty's fading flower
   Grows ever fresh with her in heavenly wise;
It had been well that she were fair of face,
And yet not rob all other dames of grace.

To muse in mind, how wise, how fair, how good,
   How brave, how frank, how courteous, and how true
My lady is, doth but inflame my blood
   With humours such as bid my health adieu:
Since hap always when it is clomb on high,
Doth fall full low, though erst it reached the sky.

Lo, pleasure, lo! lo, thus I lead a life
   That laughs for joy and trembleth oft for dread;
Thy pangs are such as call for change's knife
   To cut the twist, or else to stretch the thread,
Which holds yfeer the bundle of my bliss:
Fie, pleasure, fie! I dare not trust to this.

GEORGE GASCOIGNE

Beauty, a silver dew

Beauty, a silver dew that falls in May;
   Love is an egg-shell with that humour filled;
Desire, a wingèd boy coming that way,
   Delights and dallies with it in the field.
     The fiery sun draws up the shell on high;
     Beauty decays, love dies, desire doth fly.

ANON

Down, Wanton, Down!

Down, wanton, down! Have you no shame
That at the whisper of Love's name,
Or Beauty's, presto! up you raise
Your angry head and stand at gaze?

Poor bombard-captain, sworn to reach
The ravelin and effect a breach —
Indifferent what you storm or why,
So be that in the breach you die!

Love may be blind, but Love at least
Knows what is man and what mere beast;
Or Beauty wayward, but requires
More delicacy from her squires.

Tell me, my witless, whose one boast
Could be your staunchness at the post,
When were you made a man of parts
To think fine and profess the arts?

Will many-gifted Beauty come
Bowing to your bald rule of thumb,
Or Love swear loyalty to your crown?
Be gone, have done!   Down, wanton, down!

ROBERT GRAVES

173

Politics

How can I, that girl standing there,
My attention fix
On Roman or on Russian
Or on Spanish politics?
Yet here's a travelled man that knows
What he talks about,
And there's a politician
That has read and thought,
And maybe what they say is true
Of war and war's alarms,
But O that I were young again
And held her in my arms!

W. B. YEATS

The Ballad of
the Lonely Masturbator

The end of the affair is always death.
She's my workshop. Slippery eye,
out of the tribe of myself my breath
finds you gone. I horrify
those who stand by. I am fed.
At night, alone, I marry the bed.

Finger to finger, now she's mine.
She's not too far. She's my encounter.
I beat her like a bell. I recline
in the bower where you used to mount her.
You borrowed me on the flowered spread.
At night, alone, I marry the bed.

Take for instance this night, my love,
that every single couple puts together
with a joint overturning, beneath, above,
the abundant two on sponge and feather,
kneeling and pushing, head to head.
At night alone, I marry the bed.

I break out of my body this way,
an annoying miracle. Could I
put the dream market on display?
I am spread out. I crucify.
My little plum is what you said.
At night, alone, I marry the bed.

Then my black-eyed rival came.
The lady of water, rising on the beach,
a piano at her fingertips, shame
on her lips and a flute's speech.
And I was the knock-kneed broom instead.
At night, alone, I marry the bed.

175

She took you the way a woman takes
a bargain dress off the rack
and I broke the way a stone breaks.
I give back your books and fishing tack.
Today's paper says that you are wed.
At night, alone, I marry the bed.

The boys and girls are one tonight.
They unbutton blouses. They unzip flies.
They take off shoes. They turn off the light.
The glimmering creatures are full of lies.
They are eating each other. They are overfed.
At night, alone, I marry the bed.

ANNE SEXTON

Cuckoo

He looked with intermediate eyes
Along the lineaments of her thighs.

Man's history was just a fleeting
Moment that led to this lover's meeting.

Standing around incurious cows
Watch importunate hands invade her blouse.

The limpid air is bean blossom sweet
And her sunlit hair is a field of wheat.

The minor animal creation
Ignore this momentous copulation.

A cuckoo whistles its ribald sound
To the lovers stretched on the stony ground.

CLIFF ASHBY

BANDIED WOMEN

As Oyster Nan Stood by her Tub

As Oyster Nan stood by her tub,
   To show her vicious inclination,
She gave her noblest parts a scrub
   And sighed for want of copulation.
A vintner of no little fame
   Who excellent red and white can sell ye
Beheld the little dirty dame
   As she stood scratching of her belly.

'Come in', says he, 'you silly slut,
   'Tis now a rare convenient minute;
I'll lay the itching of your scut
   Except some greedy devil be in it.'

With that the flat-capped fubsy smiled,
   And would have blushed, but that she could
      not;
'Alas!' says she, 'we're soon beguiled
   By men to do those things we should not.'

From door they went behind the bar
   As it's by common fame reported,
And there upon a turkey chair
   Unseen the loving couple sported.
But being called by company
   As he was taking pains to please her,
'I'm coming, coming sir,' says he,
   'My dear, and so am I!' says she, sir.

Her mole-hill belly swelled about
   Into a mountain quickly after,
And when the pretty mouse crept out
   The creature caused a mighty laughter.
And now she's learned the pleasing game
   Although much pain and shame it cost her,
She daily ventures at the same
   And shuts and opens like an oyster.

ANON

181

between the breasts

between the breasts
of bestial
Marj lie large
men who praise

Marj's cleancornered strokable
body   these men's
fingers toss trunks
shuffle sacks spin kegs they

curl
loving
around
beers

the world has
these men's hands but their
bodies big and boozing
belong to

Marj
the greenslim purse of whose
face opens
on a fatgold

grin
hooray
hoorah for the large
men who lie

between the breasts
of bestial Marj
for the strong men
who

sleep between the legs of Lil

e. e. cummings

Upon My Lady Carlisle's Walking in Hampton Court Garden

Dialogue

T[HOMAS] C[AREW].   J[OHN] S[UCKLING]

Tom. Didst thou not find the place inspir'd,
And flowers, as if they had desir'd
No other sun, start from their beds,
And for a sight steal out their heads?
Heard'st thou not music when she talk'd?
And didst not find that as she walk'd
She threw rare perfumes all about,
Such as bean-blossoms newly out,
Or chafed spices give? —

J. S. I must confess those perfumes, Tom,
I did not smell; nor found that from
Her passing by aught sprung up new:
The flow'rs had all their birth from you;
For I pass'd o'er the selfsame walk,
And did not find one single stalk
Of any thing that was to bring
This unknown after-after-Spring.

Tom. Dull and insensible, couldst see
A thing so near a deity
Move up and down, and feel no change?

J. S. None and so great were alike strange.
I had my thoughts, but not your way;
All are not born, sir, to the bay;
Alas! Tom, I am flesh and blood,
And was consulting how I could

183

In spite of masks and hoods descry
The parts deni'd unto the eye:
I was undoing all she wore;
And had she walk'd but one turn more,
Eve in her first state had not been
More naked, or more plainly seen.

Tom. 'Twas well for thee she left the place;
There is great danger in that face;
But hadst thou view'd her leg and thigh,
And upon that discovery
Search'd after parts that are more dear
(As fancy seldom stops so near),
No time or age had ever seen
So lost a thing as thou hadst been.

SIR JOHN SUCKLING

An Epitaph on M.H.

In this cold Monument lies one,
That I know who has lain upon,
The happier He: her Sight would charm,
And Touch have kept King David warm.
Lovely, as is the dawning East,
Was this Marble's frozen Guest;
As soft, and Snowy, as that Down
Adorns the Blow-balls frizzled Crown;
As straight and slender as the Crest,
Or Antlet of the one-beam'd Beast;
Pleasant as th'odorous Month of May:
As glorious, and as light as Day.

Whom I admir'd, as soon as knew,
And now her Memory pursue
With such a superstitious Lust,
That I could fumble with her Dust.

She all Perfections had, and more,
Tempting, as if design'd a Whore,
For so she was; and since there are
Such, I could wish them all as fair.

Pretty she was, and young, and wise,
And in her Calling so precise,
That Industry had made her prove
The sucking School-Mistress of Love:

And Death, ambitious to become
Her Pupil, left his Ghastly home,
And, seeing how we us'd her here,
The raw-bon'd Rascal ravisht her.

Who, pretty Soul, resign'd her Breath,
To seek new Lechery in Death.

CHARLES COTTON

185

On a Maid of Honour Seen by a Scholar in Somerset Garden

As once in black I disrespected walked,
Where glittering courtiers in their Tissues stalked,
I cast by chance my melancholy eye
Upon a woman (as I thought) passed by.
But when I viewed her ruff, and beaver reared
As if *Priapus*-like she would have feared
The ravenous *Harpies* from the clustered grape,
Then I began much to mistrust her shape;
When viewing curiously, away she slipped,
And in a fount her whited hand she dipped,
The angry water as if wrong'd thereby,
Ran murmuring thence a second touch to fly,
At which away she stalks, and as she goes
She views the situation of each rose;
And having higher rais'd her gown, she gaz'd
Upon her crimson stocking which amaz'd
Blusht at her open impudence, and sent
Reflection to her cheek, for punishment.
As thus I stood the Gardener chance to pass,
My friend (quoth I) what is this stately lass?
A maid of honour Sir, said he, and goes
Leaving a riddle, was enough to pose
The crafty *Œdipus*, for I could see
Nor maid, nor honour, sure no honesty.

THOMAS RANDOLPH?

Bonny Black Bess

Methinks the poor town has been troubled too long
With Phyllis and Chloris in every song,
By fools who at once can both love and despair,
And will never leave calling them cruel and fair;
Which justly provokes me in rhyme to express
The truth that I know of bonny Black Bess.

This Bess of my heart, this Bess of my soul,
Has a skin white as milk and hair black as coal;
She 's plump, yet with ease you may span round her
     waist,
But her round swelling thighs can scarce be embraced:
Her belly is soft, not a word of the rest,
But I know what I think when I drink to the best.

The ploughman and squire, the arranter clown,
At home she subdued in her paragon gown;
But now she adorns the boxes and pit,
And the proudest town-gallants are forced to submit;
All hearts fall a-leaping wherever she comes,
And beat day and night, like my Lord Craven's drums.

I dare not permit her to come to Whitehall,
For she 'd outshine the ladies, paint, jewels, and all;
If a lord should but whisper his love in the crowd,
She 'd sell him a bargain, and laugh out aloud;
Then the Queen, overhearing what Betty did say,
Would send Mr Roper to take her away.

But to these that have had my dear Bess in their arms,
She 's gentle, and knows how to soften her charms;
And to every beauty can add a new grace,
Having learned how to lisp and to trip in her pace,
And, with head on one side and a languishing eye,
To kill *us* by looking as if *she* would die.

CHARLES SACKVILLE, EARL OF DORSET

Muirland Meg

Among our young lassies there's Muirland Meg,
She'll beg or she work, and she'll play or she beg,
At thirteen her maidenhead flew to the gate,
And the door o' her cage stands open yet. —

Her kittle black een they wad thirl you thro'.
Her rose-bud lips cry, kiss me now;
The curls and links o' her bonie black hair, —
Wad put you in mind that the lassie has mair. —

An armfu' o' love is her bosom sae plump,
A span o' delight is her middle sae jimp;
A taper, white leg, and a thumpin thie,
And a fiddle near by, an ye play a wee! —

Love's her delight, and kissin's her treasure;
She'll stick at nae price, and ye gie her gude measure,
As lang's a sheep-fit, and as girt's a goose-egg,
And that's the measure o' Muirland Meg.

ANON/ROBERT BURNS

The Bonniest Lass

The bonniest lass that ye meet neist
   Gie her a kiss an' a' that,
In spite o' ilka parish priest,
   Repentin' stool, an' a' that.

     For a' that an' a' that,
       Their mim-mou'd sangs an' a' that,
     In time and place convenient,
       They'll do't themselves for a' that.

Your patriarchs in days o' yore,
   Had their handmaids an' a' that;
O' bastard gets, some had a score
   An' some had mair than a' that.

     For a' that an' a' that,
       Your langsyne saunts, an' a' that,
     Were fonder o' a bonie lass,
       Than you or I, for a' that.

King Davie, when he waxed auld,
   An's bluid ran thin, an' a' that,
An' fand his cods were growin' cauld,
   Could not refrain, for a' that.

     For a' that an' a' that,
       To keep him warm an' a' that
     The daughters o' Jerusalem
       Were waled for him, an' a' that.

Wha wadna pity thae sweet dames
   He fumbled at, an' a' that,
An' raised their bluid up into flames
   He couldna drown, for a' that.

For a' that an' a' that,
   He wanted pith, an' a' that;
For, as to what we shall not name,
   What could he do but claw that.

King Solomon, prince o' divines,
   Wha proverbs made, an' a' that,
Baith mistresses an' concubines
   In hundreds had, for a' that.

   For a' that an' a' that,
      Tho' a preacher wise an' a' that,
   The smuttiest sang that e'er was sung
      His Sang o' Sangs is a' that.

Then still I swear, a clever chiel
   Should kiss a lass, an' a' that,
Tho' priests consign him to the deil,
   As reprobate, an' a' that.

   For a' that an' a' that,
      Their canting stuff, an' a' that,
   They ken nae mair wha's reprobate
      Than you or I, for a' that.

ROBERT BURNS

Our John's Brak Yestreen

Twa neebor wives sat i' the sun,
  A twynin' at their rocks,
An' they an argument began,
  An' a' the plea was c — ks.

'Twas whether they were sinnens strang,
  Or whether they were bane?
An' how they row'd about your thumb,
  And how they stan't themlane?

First, Raichie gae her rock a rug,
  An' syne she claw'd her tail;
'When our Tam draws on his breeks,
  'It waigles like a flail.'

Says Bess, 'they're bane I will maintain,
  'And proof in han' I'll gie;
'For our John's it brak yestreen,
  'And the margh ran down my thie.'

ROBERT BURNS?

margh: marrow (i.e. sperm)

Judith

Holofernes had meant to enjoy Judith;
She would have the laugh of him (he said) if he did not.
She sat upon spread skins and ate daintily
While he admired the spectacle for too long.
I put it down to his being a great captain,
Which made the world seem easy to him: while he stared
He grew drunk and then completely insensible.
After that she had only to cut off his head
And took it home folded up in a cloth.
She understood the place of love among
The larger affairs of the world
And was, you may say, a domesticated woman.

C. H. SISSON

For Ann

A woman of quality
Is not created
Whole or wholesome,
And passes through the madness
God prescribes for those
Intent upon eternal knowledge.
   A woman of quality
Learns to lie and cheat,
Becomes an artist in chicanery,
Holding her love like cards
Against her breast
Wanting to trump
Everybody's aces,
Yet never believes she can be loved
And makes demands
Beyond man's frail ability.
   A woman of quality
Learns through guilt
The secrets of the heart,
Wearing her two black eyes
Like bright and shining stars.
   A woman of quality can say
'It was as much my fault as yours,'
And kiss the drunken fist so full of folly.
   A woman of quality
Asks for nothing, forgives all
And is imperfect, but aware
In the shattering hours of night
Of the holiness of life.

The imperfections of man are revealed
When I can no longer love you
And have forgotten the ecstasy we suffered
Because your neck grows scraggy.
Yet seeing you lost and lonely
In the gaiety of the crowded hall
Am overcome by memories and grief.

CLIFF ASHBY

from *Reminiscences of Norma*

It is well for you tonight pretty girl
To put on your dancing stockings and twirl twirl
In exquisite clubs of drink and lust
While I rack myself with jealous thoughts
Of brute sailors smirking
And your crushed self finding in their tattooed arms
More sweetness than in my foolish love.

Or perhaps an ambitious clerk,
The facets of his face gleaming in subdued light
Is at this moment subjecting you
To an expensive obscene ritual
From which your joy in his concentration
(Which excludes you completely),
Excludes your lover.

Or perhaps you are seducing someone comically,
Whom 'you quite like really', in a taxi:
A sick columnist who lives on pills
And celebrates, rolling naked to Wagner,
The supremacy of white rulers.

Or perhaps in teenage coffee-bars
With black discs in front of your eyes
You are committing welfare;
Yearning later to taste their contempt
And to be robbed of your awful love —
A mystery in which your lover has no share.

So in my imagined bitterness,
I, who have no rights over you whatever,
And who abuse you with such thoughts,
Jealously writhe.

Yet how can I believe
That when you take down your hair
And come to me smiling
Your heart is not there?

*   *   *

I met you, Norma, dearly young,
In scented night. Though you spoke of wars
Between men and women, of alternate triumphs,
I noticed the trees only, ghostly-green
In dark. Your youth excited my mind,
My eyes were fixed, I did not dare to think
So much for your embrace I longed.
You were so fair
You would not lead me home until sun shone.

The flies were busy round desire
Before you drew me in. I eyed
The crossed dildoes on your walls,
The sex-stained trophies
The splendid images of death;
In my own first gruntings heard the buzzings of decay
On the tender face of that amorous day;
Wanted to stay.

I tried to be decent in our sty;
Found pleasure gave
Sense back to my eye:
While you lolled into rest
I saw that you were older than I thought
And knew you as a witherer of green,
Obscene
And rotting Helen of all wars never won.

Yet for passion I strained on:
Your stench was that of the divine.
Now you are silent I miss your mind,
Lack the stink of your vanished rind.
Oh how long in your palace will I lust alone
For bones whose flesh so long ago I wronged?

*   *   *

I left you Norma and you died alone
In that room whose ancient pieces stopped the sun.
Then from the street towards you there crept one
To wash your body lying on our dark bed:
To sponge your thighs still filthy with my sperm
And kiss pale lips that once were red and firm.
It was the ghost of me who grieving left
At dusk: my Christ-half's turn of cheek away
From me. I could not refuse its gift

And all my lightness now is filled with pain:
As you rise in my mind, so lusty and so gay.
I left you once, but now be mine to hold,
For memory warms what only real is cold!

MARTIN SEYMOUR-SMITH

PLIGHT

Died of love

A brisk young lover came a-courting me,
He stole away my liberty.
He stole it away with a free good will,
And though he's false, I love him still.

All in the meadows and I did run,
A-gathering flowers as they sprung;
Of every sort I plucked and pulled
Until I got my apron full.

When I wore my apron low,
My love followed me through frost and snow;
But when I wore it up to my chin,
My love passed by and never looked in.

There is a bird in yonder tree;
Some say he's blind and cannot see.
I wish it had been the same with me
Before I gained his company.

I wish to God my babe was born,
Sat smiling on its daddy's arms,
And I myself all in the cold clay
And the green grass growing over me.

There is an ale house in yonder town,
Where my love goes and sits him down;
He takes some strange girl on his knee
And tells her what he doesn't tell me.

A grief to me and I'll tell you why:
Because she's got more gold than I.
Her gold will waste and her beauty pass
And she will come like me at last.

ANON

201

The Nightingale

Jug, jug! Fair fall the nightingale,
   Whose tender breast
Chants out her merry madrigal,
   With hawthorn pressed:
Te'u, te'u! thus sings she even by even,
And represents the melody in heaven:
     Tis, tis,
    I am not as I wish.

Rape-defilëd Philomel
   In her sad mischance
Tells what she is forced to tell,
   While the satyrs dance:
'Unhappy I,' quoth she, 'unhappy I,
That am betrayed by Tereus' treachery;
     Tis, tis,
    I am not as I wish.

'Chaste-unchaste, deflowered, yet
   Spotless in heart,
Lust was all that he could get,
   For all his art:
For I ne'er attention lent
To his suit, nor gave consent;
     Tis, tis,
    I am not as I wish.'

Thus hath faithless Tereus made
  Heartless Philomele
Moan her in her forlorn shade,
  Where grief I feel —
Grief that wounds me to the heart,
Which though gone hath left her smart;
    Tis, tis,
  I am not as I wish.

RICHARD BRATHWAITE

What Can We Poor Females Do

What can we poor females do,
When pressing teasing lovers sue?
Fate affords no other way
   But denying, or complying;
   And resenting, or consenting,
Does alike our hopes betray.

ANON

SATIRICAL

Wake all the dead

Wake all the dead! what ho! what ho!
How soundly they sleep whose pillows lie low!
They mind not poor lovers who walk above
On the decks of the world in storms of love.
 No whisper now nor glance can pass
 Through wickets or through panes of glass;
For our windows and doors are shut and barred.
Lie close in the church and in the churchyard.
 In every grave make room, make room!
 The world's at an end, and we come, we come.

The state is now love's foe, love's foe;
Has seized on his arms, his quiver and bow;
Has pinioned his wings, and fettered his feet,
Because he made way for lovers to meet.
 But O sad chance, his judge was old;
 Hearts cruel grow when blood grows cold.
No man being young his process would draw.
O heavens, that love should be subject to law!
 Lovers go woo the dead, the dead!
 Lie two in a grave, and to bed, to bed!

SIR WILLIAM DAVENANT

The Candle

There is a thing which in the light
Is seldom used; but in the night
It serves the maiden female crew,
The ladies, and the good-wives too:
They use to take it in their hand,
And then it will uprightly stand;
And to a hole they it apply,
Where by its goodwill it would die;
It spends, goes out, and still within
It leaves its moisture thick and thin.

SIR JOHN SUCKLING

On Sir Voluptuous Beast

While BEAST instructs his fair and innocent wife,
In the past pleasures of his sensual life,
Telling the motions of each petticoat,
And how his Ganymede moved, and how his goat,
And now her hourly her own cucquean makes,
In varied shapes, which for his lust she takes:
What doth he else, but say Leave to be chaste,
Just wife, and to change me, make woman's haste!

*   *   *

On the Same Beast

Than his chaste wife though BEAST now know no
    more,
He adulters still: his thoughts lie with a whore.

BEN JONSON

On a Pair of Garters

Go, loving woodbine, clip with lovely grace
Those two sweet plants which bear the flowers of love.
Go, silken vines, those tender elms embrace
Which flourish still, although their roots do move.
As soon as you possess your blessed places
You are advancèd and ennobled more
Than diadems, which were white silken laces
That ancient kings about their forehead wore.
Sweet bands, take heed lest you ungently bind,
Or with your strictness make too deep a print:
Was never tree had such a tender rind,
Although her inward heart be hard as flint.
    And let your knots be fast and loose at will:
    She must be free, though I stand bound and still.

SIR JOHN DAVIES

Signior Dildo

You ladies all of merry England
Who have been to kiss the Duchess's hand,
Pray, did you lately observe in the show
A noble Italian called Signior Dildo?

This signior was one of Her Highness's train,
And helped to conduct her over the main;
But now she cries out, 'To the Duke I will go!
I have no more need for Signior Dildo.'

At the Sign of the Cross in St James's Street,
When next you go thither to make yourselves
    sweet
By buying of powder, gloves, essence, or so,
You may chance t' get a sight of Signior Dildo.

You'll take him at first for no person of note
Because he appears in a plain leather coat,
But when you his virtuous abilities know,
You'll fall down and worship Signior Dildo.

My Lady Southesk, heavens prosper her for 't!
First clothed him in satin, then brought him to
    Court;
But his head in the circle he scarcely durst show,
So modest a youth was Signior Dildo.

The good Lady Suffolk, thinking no harm,
Had got this poor stranger hid under her arm.
Lady Betty by chance came the secret to know,
And from her own mother stole Signior Dildo.

The Countess of Falmouth, of whom people tell
Her footmen wear shirts of a guinea an ell,

Duchess's: the Duchess of Modena, who had just married
    James, Duke of York, the future James II

Might save the expense if she did but know
How lusty a swinger is Signior Dildo.

By the help of this gallant the countess of Ralph
Against the fierce Harrys preserved herself safe.
She stifled him almost beneath her pillow,
So closely sh' embraced Signior Dildo.

Our dainty fine duchesses have got a trick
To dote on a fool for the sake of his prick:
The fops were undone, did Their Graces but know
The discretion and vigor of Signior Dildo.

That pattern of virtue, Her Grace of Cleveland,
Has swallowed more pricks than the ocean has sand;
But by rubbing and scrubbing so large it does grow,
It is fit for just nothing but Signior Dildo.

The Duchess of Modena, though she looks high,
With such a gallant is contented to lie,
And for fear the English her secrets should know,
For a Gentleman Usher took Signior Dildo.

The countess o' th' Cockpit (Who knows not her name?
She's famous in story for a killing dame),
When all her old lovers forsake her, I trow
She'll then be contented with Signior Dildo.

Red Howard, red Sheldon, and Temple so tall
Complain of his absence so long from Whitehall;
Signior Bernard has promised a journey to go
And bring back his countryman Signior Dildo.

Doll Howard no longer with 's Highness must range,
And therefore is proffered this civil exchange:

Her teeth being rotten, she smells best below,
And needs must be fitted for Signior Dildo.

St Albans, with wrinkles and smiles in his face,
Whose kindness to strangers becomes his high place,
In his coach and six horses is gone to Borgo
To take the fresh air with Signior Dildo.

Were this signior but known to the citizen fops,
He'd keep their fine wives from the foremen of shops;
But the rascals deserve their horns should still grow
For burning the Pope and his nephew Dildo.

Tom Killigrew's wife, north Holland's fine flower,
At the sight of this signior did fart and belch sour,
And her Dutch breeding farther to show,
Says, 'Welcome to England, Mynheer Van Dildo!'

He civilly came to the Cockpit one night,
And proffered his service to fair Madam Knight.
Quoth she, 'I intrigue with Captain Cazzo;
Your nose in mine arse, good Signior Dildo!'

This signior is sound, safe, ready, and dumb
As ever was candle, carrot, or thumb;
Then away with these nasty devices, and show
How you rate the just merits of Signior Dildo.

Count Cazzo, who carries his nose very high,
In passion he swore his rival should die;
Then shut up himself to let the world know
Flesh and blood could not bear it from Signior Dildo.

Cazzo: colloquial Italian for 'penis'

A rabble of pricks who were welcome before,
Now finding the Porter denied 'em the door,
Maliciously waited his coming below
And inhumanly fell on Signior Dildo.

Nigh wearied out, the poor stranger did fly,
And along the Pall Mall they followed full cry;
The women, concerned, from every window
Cried, 'Oh! for heavens' sake, save Signior Dildo!'

The good Lady Sandys burst into a laughter
To see how the ballocks came wobbling after,
And had not their weight retarded the foe,
Indeed 't had gone hard with Signior Dildo.

JOHN WILMOT, EARL OF ROCHESTER

French Lisette:
A Ballad of Maida Vale

Who strolls so late, for mugs a bait,
In the mists of Maida Vale,
Sauntering past a stucco gate
Fallen, but hardly frail?

You can safely bet that it's French Lisette,
The pearl of Portsdown Square,
On the game she has made her name
And rather more than her share.

In a coat of cony with her passport phony
She left her native haunts,
For an English surname exchanging *her* name
And then took up with a ponce.

Now a meaning look conceals the hook
Some innocent fish will swallow,
Chirping 'Hullo, Darling!' like a cheeky starling
She'll turn, and he will follow,

For her eyes are blue and her eyelids too
And her smile's by no means cryptic,
Her perm's as firm as if waved with glue,
She plies an orange lipstick,

And orange-red is her perky head
Under a hat like a tiny pie —
A pie on a tart, it might be said,
Is redundant, but oh, how spry!

From the distant tundra to snuggle under her
Chin a white fox was conveyed,
And with winks and leerings and Woolworth
    earrings
She's all set up for trade.

Now who comes here replete with beer?
A quinquagenarian clerk
Who in search of Life has left 'the wife'
And 'the kiddies' in Tufnell Park.

Dear sir, beware! for sex is a snare
And all is not true that allures.
Good sir, come off it! She means to profit
By this little weakness of yours:

Too late for alarm! Exotic charm
Has caught in his gills like a gaff,
He goes to his fate with a hypnotized gait,
The slave of her silvery laugh,

And follows her in to her suite of sin,
Her self-contained bower of bliss,
They enter her flat, she takes his hat,
And he hastens to take a kiss.

Ah, if only he knew that concealed from view
Behind a 'folk-weave' curtain
Is her fancy man, called Dublin Dan,
His manner would be less certain,

His bedroom eyes would express surprise,
His attitude less languor,
He would watch his money, not call her 'Honey',
And be seized with fear or anger.

Of the old technique one need scarcely speak,
But oh, in the quest for Romance
'Tis folly abounding in a strange surrounding
To be divorced from one's pants.

WILLIAM PLOMER

A Ramble in St James's Park

Much wine had passed, with grave discourse
Of who fucks who, and who does worse
(Such as you usually do hear
From those that diet at the Bear),
When I, who still take care to see
Drunkenness relieved by lechery,
Went out into St James's Park
To cool my head and fire my heart.
But though St James has th' honour on 't,
'Tis consecrate to prick and cunt.
There, by a most incestuous birth,
Strange woods spring from the teeming earth;
For they relate how heretofore,
When ancient Pict began to whore,
Deluded of his assignation
(Jilting, it seems, was then in fashion),
Poor pensive lover, in this place
Would frig upon his mother's face;
Whence rows of mandrakes tall did rise
Whose lewd tops fucked the very skies.
Each imitative branch does twine
In some loved fold of Aretine,
And nightly now beneath their shade
Are buggeries, rapes, and incests made.
Unto this all-sin-sheltering grove
Whores of the bulk and the alcove,
Great ladies, chambermaids, and drudges,
The ragpicker, and heiress trudges.
Carmen, divines, great lords, and tailors,
Prentices, poets, pimps, and jailers,
Footmen, fine fops do here arrive,
And here promiscuously they swive.
   Along these hallowed walks it was
That I beheld Corinna pass.

Aretine: Pietro Aretino: Italian author who had written obscene
poems

Whoever had been by to see
The proud disdain she cast on me
Through charming eyes, he would have swore
She dropped from heaven that very hour,
Forsaking the divine abode
In scorn of some despairing god.
But mark what creatures women are:
How infinitely vile, when fair!
 Three knights o' th' elbow and the slur
With wriggling tails made up to her.
 The first was of your Whitehall blades,
Near kin t' th' Mother of the Maids;
Graced by whose favour he was able
To bring a friend t' th' Waiters' table,
Where he had heard Sir Edward Sutton
Say how the King loved Banstead mutton;
Since when he'd ne'er be brought to eat
By 's good will any other meat.
In this, as well as all the rest,
He ventures to do like the best,
But wanting common sense, th' ingredient
In choosing well not least expedient,
Converts abortive imitation
To universal affectation.
Thus he not only eats and talks
But feels and smells, sits down and walks,
Nay looks, and lives, and loves by rote,
In an old tawdry birthday coat.
 The second was a Grays Inn wit,
A great inhabiter of the pit,
Where critic-like he sits and squints,
Steals pocket handkerchiefs, and hints,
From 's neighbour, and the comedy,
To court, and pay, his landlady.

Knights o' the elbow: cheats   *slur*: method of fixing dice

The third, a lady's eldest son
Within few years of twenty-one,
Who hopes from his propitious fate,
Against he comes to his estate,
By these two worthies to be made
A most accomplished tearing blade.
  One, in a strain 'twixt tune and nonsense,
Cries, 'Madam, I have loved you long since.
Permit me your fair hand to kiss';
When at her mouth her cunt cries, 'Yes!'
In short, without much more ado,
Joyful and pleased, away she flew,
And with these three confounded asses
From park to hackney coach she passes.
  So a proud bitch does lead about
Of humble curs the amorous rout,
Who most obsequiously do hunt
The savoury scent of salt-swoln cunt.
Some power more patient now relate
The sense of this surprising fate.
Gods! that a thing admired by me
Should fall to so much infamy.
Had she picked out, to rub her arse on,
Some stiff-pricked clown or well-hung parson,
Each job of whose spermatic sluice
Had filled her cunt with wholesome juice,
I the proceeding should have praised
In hope sh' had quenched a fire I raised.
Such natural freedoms are but just:
There's something generous in mere lust.
But to turn damned abandoned jade
When neither head nor tail persuade;
To be a whore in understanding,
A passive pot for fools to spend in!
The devil played booty, sure, with thee

To bring a blot on infamy.
  But why am I, of all mankind,
To so severe a fate designed?
Ungrateful! Why this treachery
To humble, fond, believing me,
Who gave you privilege above
The nice allowances of love?
Did ever I refuse to bear
The meanest part your lust could spare?
When your lewd cunt came spewing home
Drenched with the seed of half the town,
My dram of sperm was supped up after
For the digestive surfeit water.
Full gorgèd at another time
With a vast meal of nasty slime
Which your devouring cunt had drawn
From porters' backs and footmen's brawn,
I was content to serve you up
My ballock-full for your grace cup,
Nor ever thought it an abuse
While you had pleasure for excuse —
You that could make my heart away
For noise and colour, and betray
The secrets of my tender hours
To such knight-errant paramours,
When, leaning on your faithless breast,
Wrapped in security and rest,
Soft kindness all my powers did move,
And reason lay dissolved in love!
  May stinking vapours choke your womb
Such as the men you dote upon!
May your depravèd appetite,
That could in whiffling fools delight,
Beget such frenzies in your mind
You may go mad for the north wind,

And fixing all your hopes upon 't
To have him bluster in your cunt,
Turn up your longing arse t' th' air
And perish in a wild despair!
But cowards shall forget to rant,
Schoolboys to frig, old whores to paint;
The Jesuits' fraternity
Shall leave the use of buggery;
Crab-louse, inspired with grace divine,
From earthly cod to heaven shall climb;
Physicians shall believe in Jesus,
And disobedience cease to please us,
Ere I desist with all my power
To plague this woman and undo her.
But my revenge will best be timed
When she is married that is limed.
In that most lamentable state
I'll make her feel my scorn and hate:
Pelt her with scandals, truth or lies,
And her poor cur with jealousies,
Till I have torn him from her breech,
While she whines like a dog-drawn bitch;
Loathed and despised, kicked out o' th' Town
Into some dirty hole alone,
To chew the cud of misery
And know she owes it all to me.
   And may no woman better thrive
   That dares prophane the cunt I swive!

JOHN WILMOT, EARL OF ROCHESTER

The Universal Prayer

Mother of all! in ev'ry age,
    In ev'ry Clime ador'd,
By Saint, by Savage, and by Sage,
    If modest, or if whor'd

Thou great first Cause, least understood,
    Who all my Prick confin'd;
To feel but this, that thou art good,
    And that himself is blind.

You gave him in this dark Estate
    To know the Good from Ill;
With godlike Virtue to create,
    Following his Prickship's Will.

Sound, honest Cunts should oft be done,
    Unsound I ne'er would do;
There teach me more than hell to shun,
    Those more than Heav'n pursue.

What Seed my God's free Bounty gives,
    Let me not frig away;
For God is paid when Cunt receives,
    T'enjoy is to obey.

Yet not one Cunt's contracted Span
    My Vigour e'er shall bound;
I think they all were made for Man,
    When thousand Cunts were round.

If I am clapt, may this Right-hand
    Its happy Cunning know;
Let rankling Venom round the Land
    Brand Pego as a foe.

If he goes right, thy Grace impart,
    Still in the Right to stay;
Oh! may he ne'er from Thee depart,
    To find the Primate's way.

Save him alike from foolish Pride,
    Or impious Discontent;
If greater thickness be denied,
    Or thirteen inches lent.

Teach me to feed a Virgin's Woe,
    The Maiden Gore I see,
In sacred Drops from Hymen flow,
    Be kiss'd and wip'd by me.

Mean tho' my Prick, not wholly so
    Since stiff'd by thy Breath;
Oh! lead him where he ought to go
    In this Night's Life or Death.

This Night be thou black-hair'd my Lot;
    Or else beneath the Sun,
God knows if best bestow'd or not,
    But let thy Work be done

To thee whose Fucks thro'out all space,
    This dying World supplies,
One Chorus let all Beings raise!
    All Pricks in rev'rence rife

JOHN WILKES

The Universal Prayer parodies a famous hymn

The Dying Lover to his Prick

Happy Spark of heavenly Flame!
    Pride and Wonder of Man's Frame!
    Why is Pleasure so soon flying?
    Why so short this Bliss of dying?
Cease, fond Pego, cease the Strife,
And yet indulge a Moment's Life.
    Hark, Cunt whispers, don't she stay,
    Brother Pego come away?
    What is this aborts me quite,
    Steals my Senses, shuts my sight;
Drowns my Spirits, draws my Breath?
Tell me, my Prick, can this be Death?
    Now you recede, now disappear!
    My Eye looks round in Vain, my Ear;
    Fanny, your Murmur rings:
    Lend, lend your Hand! I mount! I die!
    O Prick, how great thy Victory?
    O Pleasure! sweet thy Stings.

JOHN WILKES

The Dying Lover to his Prick: parodies 'The Dying Christian's Prayer to his Soul'

Planning Permission

He looked at me without surprise or pleasure
But with a bored, habitual compassion.
'They sent me here,' I said. 'I want to build.'
'Naturally,' he said. 'We'll see what we can do.'
Along the hopeless counter twenty others
Were seeing what they could do.
                         'You'll need these forms.'
Application for permission for an erection
For occupation as residential accommodation
And/or private domestic habitation.
'In triplicate of course. Return when filled
To the assistant sub-divisional officer.'
I took the papers. Tears of gratitude
Misted my sight; but he was gone already
Into the wastes beneath his sandy hair.

I took the papers back.
Alone in his little room
The assistant sub-divisional officer sent for me.
He looked at me without surprise or pleasure
But with compassionate unrecognition.
'Permission for an erection. Quite so. We'll write.'
'Oh thank you, sir,' I started. 'Do you think . . . ?'
But under the sandy hair the eyes were blank.
After eleven months the answer came.
'Rejection of permission for an erection.
Any appeal to be directed within three years
To the sub-divisional officer for attention.'

Two years and more went by before I gained
The sub-divisional officer's section. With relief
I saw that he at least had had his due reward.
Between the flat ears under the greying hair
No sign of recognition stirred.
                             'Ah yes.

Objection to rejection of application for erection.'
With the old bored compassion in his voice,
'We'll do,' he promised, 'what we can to help.'
'Oh sir,' I sobbed. He interrupted me.
'I'll pass on your objection to the divisional officer.
It may take time.'
                    Re-charged with hope I went.

I died; and here I falter by the gate
Drained of desire and too ashamed to face
The sorrowing figure on the throne of grace.

                                        JAMES REEVES

WHORING

The Harlot

It is the body of the young harlot
Somewhere, I forget just where I saw it —
Above a doorway of the cathedral at Chartres
Or it might have been at Rheims —
Naked and beautiful, a very human beauty
And therefore a beauty whose meaning is pity,
Carried shoulder-high
By the hawk-headed demons.

The long hair, the face tilted up to the sky
As if waiting for rain to fall,
The breasts, the bone cage of the ribs,
The soft pouch of generation,
The collarbone — yes, the collarbone in particular —
And her arms hanging slack
Like someone carried on a bier.

'I thought you might be here', she said,
And smiled the broad smile I had seen before.

JAMES K. BAXTER

The Ramble

While Duns were knocking at my Door,
I lay in Bed with reeking Whore,
With Back so weak and Prick so sore,
                You'd wonder.

I rous'd my Doe, and lac'd her Gown,
I pin'd her Whisk, and dropt a Crown,
She pist, and then I drove her down,
                Like Thunder.

From Chamber then I went to dinner,
I drank small Beer like mournful Sinner,
And still I thought the Devil in her
                Clitoris.

I sat at Muskat's in the dark,
I heard a Trades-man and a Spark,
An Attorney and a Lawyer's Clark,
                Tell Stories.

From thence I went, with muffled Face,
To the Duke's House, and took a place,
In which I spew'd, may't please his Grace,
                Or Highness.

Shou'd I been hang'd I could not choose
But laugh at Whores that drop from Stews,
Seeing that Mistress Marg'ret Hewghs
                So fine is.

When Play was done, I call'd a Link;
I heard some paltry pieces chink
Within my Pockets, how d'ee think
                I'employ'd 'em?

Whoring

Why, Sir, I went to Mistress Spering,
Where some were cursing, others swearing,
Never a Barrel better Herring,
                              Per fidem.

Seven's the main, 'tis Eight, God dam' me,
'Twas six, said I, as God shall sa' me,
Now being true you cou'd not blame me
                              So saying.

Sa' me! quoth one, what Shamaroon
Is this, has begg'd an Afternoon
Of's Mother, to go up and down
                              A playing?

This was as bad to me as killing,
Mistake not Sir, said I, I'm willing,
And able both, to drop a shilling,
                              Or two Sir.

Goda'mercy then, said Bully Hec-
With Whiskers stern, and Cordubeck
Pinn'd up behind his scabby neck
                              To shew Sir.

With mangled fist he grasp'd the Box,
Giving the Table bloody knocks,
He throws — and calls for Plague and Pox
                              T'assist him.

Some twenty shillings he did catch,
H'ad like t'have made a quick dispatch,
Nor could, Time's Register, my Watch
                              Have missed him.

As Luck would have it, in came Will,
Perceiving things went very ill,
Quoth he, y'ad better go and swill

Canary.

We steer'd our course to Dragon Green,
Which is in Fleetstreet to be seen,
Where we drank Wine — not foul — but clean

Contrary.

Our Host, y'cleped Thomas Hammond,
Presented slice of Bacon Gammon,
Which made us swallow Sack as Salmon

Drink water.

Being o'er-warm'd with last debauch,
I grew as drunk as any Roch,
When hot-bak'd-Wardens did approach,

Or later.

But oh! the damn'd confounded Fate
Attends on drinking Wine so late,
I drew my Sword on honest Kate

O'th'Kitchen;

Which Hammond's Wife would not endure,
I told her tho' she look'd demure,
She came but lately I was sure

From Bitching.

We broke the Glasses out of hand,
As many Oaths I'd at command
As Hastings, Sabin, Sunderland,

Or Ogle.

Whoring

Then I cry'd up Sir Henry Vane,
And swore by God I would maintain
Episcopacy was too plain

        A juggle.

And having now discharg'd the House,
We did reserve a gentle Souse,
With which we drank another rouse

        At the Bar.

And now good Christians all attend,
To Drunkenness pray put an end,
I do advise you as a Friend,

        And Neighbour.

For lo! that Mortal here behold,
Who cautious was in days of old,
Is now become rash, sturdy, bold,

        And free Sir;

For having scap'd the Tavern so,
There never was a greater Foe,
Encounter'd yet by Pompey, No

        Nor Cæsar:

A Constable both stern and dread,
Who is from Mustard, Brooms and Thread,
Preferr'd to be the Brainless Head —

        O'th'People.

A Gown 'had on by Age made grey,
A Hat too, which as Folk do say,
Is surnam'd to this very day

        A Steeple.

His Staff, which knew as well as he,
The Bus'ness of Authority,
Stood bold upright at sight of me;
     Very true 'tis.

Those lousy Curs that hither come
To keep the King's Peace safe at home,
Yet cannot keep the Vermin from
     Their Cutis.

Stand! stand! says one, and come before —
You lie, said I, like a Son of a Whore,
I can't, nor will not stand, — that's more —
     D'ye mutter?

You watchful Knaves, I'll tell you what,
Yond' Officer i'th May-pole Hat,
I'll make as drunk as any Rat,
     Or Otter.

The Constable began to swell,
Altho' he lik'd the motion well:
Quoth he, my Friend, this I must tell
     Ye clearly,

The Pestilence you can't forget,
Nor the Dispute with Dutch, nor yet
The dreadful Fire, that made us get
     Up early.

From which, quoth he, this I infer,
To have a Body's Conscience clear,
Excelleth any costly cheer,
     Or Banquets.

Dispute with Dutch: the Dutch War then going on
dreadful Fire of London

Besides, (and 'faith I think he wept)
Were it not better you had kept
Within your Chamber, and have slept
                    In Blanquets?

But I'll advise you by and by;
A Pox of all advise, said I,
Your Janizaries look as dry
            As Vulcan:

Come, here's a shilling, fetch it in,
We come not now to talk of Sin,
Our Bus'ness must be to begin
            A full Can.

At last, I made the Watch-men drunk,
Examin'd here and there a Punk,
And then away to Bed I slunk
            To hide it.

God save the Queen! — but as for you,
Who will these Dangers not eschew,
I'd have you all go home and spew
            As I did.

ALEXANDER RADCLIFFE

The Women's Complaint to Venus

How happy were good English Faces
    Till Monsieur from France
    Taught Pego a Dance
To the tune of old Sodom's Embraces.

But now we are quite out of Fashion:
    Poor Whores may be Nuns
    Since Men turn their Guns
And vent on each other their passion.

In the Reign of good Charles the Second
    Full many a Jade
    A Lady was made
And the Issue Right Noble was reckon'd:

But now we find to our Sorrow
    We are overrun
    By Sparks of the Bum
And peers of the Land of Gomorrah.

The Beaux too, whom most we reli'd on
    At Night make a punk
    Of him that's first drunk
Tho' unfit for the Sport as John Dryden.

The Soldiers, whom next we put trust in,
    No widow can tame
    Or virgin reclaim
But at the wrong Place will be thrusting.

Fair Venus, Thou Goddess of Beauty,
    Receive our Complaint
    Make Rigby Recant
And the Soldiers henceforth do their duty.

ANON

The Fornicator

Ye jovial boys who love the joys,
  The blissful joys of Lovers,
Yet dare avow, with dauntless brow,
  When the bony lass discovers,
I pray draw near, and lend an ear,
  And welcome in a Frater,
For I've lately been on quarantine,
  A proven Fornicator.

Before the Congregation wide,
  I passed the muster fairly,
My handsome Betsy by my side,
  We gat our ditty rarely;
But my downcast eye did chance to spy
  What made my lips to water,
Those limbs so clean where I between
  Commenc'd a Fornicator.

With rueful face and signs of grace
  I pay'd the buttock-hire,
But the night was dark and thro' the park
  I could not but convoy her;
A parting kiss, I could not less,
  My vows began to scatter,
My Betsy fell — lal de dal lal lal,
  I am a Fornicator.

But for her sake this vow I make,
  And solemnly I swear it,
That while I own a single crown
  She's welcome for to share it;

And my roguish boy his Mother's joy
    And the darling of his Pater,
For him I boast my pains and cost,
    Although a Fornicator.

Ye wenching blades whose hireling jades
    Have tipt you off blue-joram,
I tell you plain, I do disdain
    To rank you in the Quorum;
But a bony lass upon the grass
    To teach her esse Mater,
And no reward but fond regard,
    O that's a Fornicator

Your warlike Kings and Heros bold,
    Great Captains and Commanders;
Your mighty Caesars fam'd of old,
    And conquering Alexanders;
In fields they fought and laurels bought,
    And bulwarks strong did batter,
But still they grac'd our noble list,
    And ranked Fornicator!!!

ROBERT BURNS

Fornicator: Burns had to do public penance in the kirk for the affair,
with Betty Paton, which he celebrates here

DISGUST

Whoever hath her wish,
thou hast thy Will

Whoever hath her wish, thou hast thy Will,
And Will to boot, and Will in overplus.
More than enough am I that vex thee still,
To thy sweet will making addition thus.
Wilt thou, whose will is large and spacious,
Not once vouchsafe to hide my will in thine?
Shall will in others seem right gracious
And in my will no fair acceptance shine?
The sea, all water, yet receives rain still
And in abundance addeth to his store;
So thou, being rich in Will, add to thy Will
One will of mine to make thy large Will more.
   Let no unkind no fair beseechers kill;
   Think all but one, and me in that one Will.

WILLIAM SHAKESPEARE

Will: Shakespeare; his and his lover's sex-organs

Th' expense of spirit
in a waste of shame

Th' expense of spirit in a waste of shame
Is lust in action; and till action, lust
Is perjur'd, murd'rous, bloody, full of blame,
Savage, extreme, rude, cruel, not to trust;
Enjoy'd no sooner but despised straight;
Past reason hunted, and no sooner had,
Past reason hated, as a swallowed bait
On purpose laid to make the taker mad;
Mad in pursuit, and in possession so;
Had, having, and in quest to have, extreme;
A bliss in proof — and prov'd, a very woe;
Before, a joy propos'd; behind, a dream.
    All this the world well knows; yet none knows
      well
    To shun the heaven that leads men to this hell.

WILLIAM SHAKESPEARE

A Beautiful Young Nymph Going to Bed

WRITTEN FOR THE HONOUR OF THE FAIR SEX

Corinna, pride of Drury Lane,
For whom no shepherd sighs in vain;
Never did Covent Garden boast
So bright a battered, strolling toast;
No drunken rake to pick her up,
No cellar where on tick to sup;
Returning at the midnight hour;
Four storeys climbing to her bower;
Then, seated on a three-legged chair,
Takes off her artificial hair:
Now, picking out a crystal eye,
She wipes it clean, and lays it by.
Her eyebrows from a mouse's hide,
Stuck on with art on either side,
Pulls off with care, and first displays 'em,
Then in a play-book smoothly lays 'em.
Now dexterously her plumpers draws,
That serve to fill her hollow jaws.
Untwists a wire; and from her gums
A set of teeth completely comes.
Pulls out the rags contrived to prop
Her flabby dugs, and down they drop.
Proceeding on, the lovely goddess
Unlaces next her steel-ribbed bodice;
Which by the operator's skill,
Press down the lumps, the hollows fill.
Up goes her hand, and off she slips
The bolsters that supply her hips.
With gentlest touch, she next explores
Her shankers, issues, running sores;
Effects of many a sad disaster,
And then to each applies a plaster.
But must, before she goes to bed,

Rub off the daubs of white and red.
And smooth the furrows in her front,
With greasy paper stuck upon't.
She takes a bolus e'er she sleeps;
And then between two blankets creeps.
With pains of love tormented lies;
Or if she chance to close her eyes,
Of Bridewell and the compter dreams,
And feels the lash, and faintly screams.
Or, by a faithless bully drawn,
At some hedge-tavern lies in pawn.
Or to Jamaica seems transported,
Alone, and by no planter courted;
Or, near Fleet Ditch's oozy brinks,
Surrounded with a hundred stinks,
Belated, seems on watch to lie,
And snap some cully passing by;
Or, struck with fear, her fancy runs
On watchmen, constables and duns,
From whom she meets with frequent rubs;
But, never from religious clubs;
Whose favour she is sure to find,
Because she pays them all in kind.

Corinna wakes. A dreadful sight!
Behold the ruins of the night!
A wicked rat her plaster stole,
Half ate, and dragged it to his hole.
The crystal eye, alas, was missed;
And Puss had on her plumpers pissed.
A pigeon picked her issue-peas,
And Shock her tresses filled with fleas.

The nymph, though in this mangled plight,
Must every morn her limbs unite.

Disgust

But how shall I describe her arts
To recollect the scattered parts?
Or show the anguish, toil, and pain,
Of gathering up herself again?
The bashful muse will never bear
In such a scene to interfere.
Corinna in the morning dizened,
Who sees, will spew; who smells, be poisoned.

JONATHAN SWIFT

The Problem

Did ever problem thus perplex,
Or more employ the female sex?
So sweet a passion, who would think,
Jove ever formed to make a stink?
The ladies vow and swear they'll try,
Whether it be a truth or lie.

Love's fire, it seems, like inward heat,
Works in my Lord by stool and sweat:
Which brings a stink from every pore,
And from behind, and from before:
Yet, what is wonderful to tell it,
None but the favourite nymph can smell it.
But now to solve the natural cause
By sober philosophic laws:
Whether all passions when in ferment,
Work out, as anger does in vermin?
So, when a weasel you torment,
You find his passion by his scent.
We read of kings, who in a fright,
Though on a throne, would fall to shite.
Beside all this deep scholars know,
That the mainstring of Cupid's bow,
Once on a time, was an ass's gut,
Now to a nobler office put,
By favour or desert preferred
From giving passage to a turd.
But still, though fixed among the stars,
Doth sympathize with human arse.
Thus, when you feel an hard-bound breech,
Conclude Love's bow-string at full stretch,
Till the kind looseness comes, and then
Conclude the bow relaxed again.

Disgust

And now the ladies all are bent
To try the great experiment;
Ambitious of a regent's heart,
Spread all their charms to catch a fart!
Watching the first unsavoury wind,
Some ply before and some behind.
My Lord, on fire amidst the dames,
Farts like a laurel in the flames.
The fair approach the speaking part,
To try the back way to his heart.
For, as when we a gun discharge,
Although the bore be ne'er so large,
Before the flame from muzzle burst,
Just at the breech it flashes first:
So from my Lord his passion broke,
He farted first, and then he spoke.

The ladies vanish in the smother,
To confer notes with one another:
And now they all agree to name
Whom each one thought the happy dame.
Quoth Neal, 'Whate'er the rest may think,
I'm sure 'twas I that smelt the stink.'
'You smelt the stink! By God, you lie,'
Quoth Ross, 'for I'll be sworn 'twas I.'
'Ladies,' quoth Levens, 'pray forbear,
Let's not fall out, we all had share;
And, by the most I can discover,
My Lord's an universal lover.'

JONATHAN SWIFT

IMPOTENCE AND ABSTENTION

Hence, away, you sirens!

Hence, away, you sirens! leave me,
And unclasp your wanton arms!
Sugared words shall ne'er deceive me,
Though thou prove a thousand charms.
    Fie, fie, forbear!
    No common snare
Could ever my affection chain:
      Your painted baits
      And poor deceits
Are all bestowed on me in vain.

I 'm no slave to such as you be;
Neither shall a snowy breast,
Wanton eye, or lip of ruby
Ever rob me of my rest.
    Go, go, display
    Your beauty's ray
To some o'ersoon enamoured swain!
      Those common wiles
      Of sighs and smiles
Are all bestowed on me in vain.

I have elsewhere vowed a duty;
Turn away thy tempting eyes!
Show not me a naked beauty:
Those impostures I despise.
    My spirit loathes
    Where gaudy clothes
And feignëd oaths may love obtain.
      I love her so,
      Whose look swears 'No,'
That all your labours will be vain.

GEORGE WITHER

Out of Sight, Out of Mind

The oftener seen, the more I lust,
  The more I lust, the more I smart,
The more I smart, the more I trust,
  The more I trust, the heavier heart,
The heavy heart breeds mine unrest,
Thy absence therefore like I best.

The rarer seen, the less in mind,
  The less in mind, the lesser pain,
The lesser pain, less grief I find,
  The lesser grief, the greater gain,
The greater gain, the merrier I,
Therefore I wish thy sight to fly.

The further off, the more I joy,
  The more I joy, the happier life,
The happier life, less hurts annoy,
  The lesser hurts, pleasure most rife,
Such pleasures rife shall I obtain
When distance doth depart us twain.

BARNABY GOOGE

Song

Four arms, two necks, one wreathing;
Two pairs of lips, one breathing;
Two hearts that multiply
Sighs interchangeably:

The thought of this confounds me,
And as I speak it wounds me.
It cannot be expressed.
Good help me, whilst I rest.

Bad stomachs have their loathing,
And oh, this all is no thing:
This 'no' with griefs both prove
Report oft turns to love.

ANON

Love is a sickness

Love is a sickness full of woes,
  All remedies refusing;
A plant that with most cutting grows,
  Most barren with best using.
    Why so?
More we enjoy it, more it dies;
  If not enjoyed, it sighing cries,
    Heigh ho!

Love is a torment of the mind,
  A tempest everlasting;
And Jove hath made it of a kind
  Not well, nor full, nor fasting.
    Why so?
More we enjoy it, more it dies;
  If not enjoyed, it sighing cries,
    Heigh ho!

SAMUEL DANIEL

Love

All love at first, like generous wine,
Ferments and frets, until 'tis fine;
But when 'tis settled on the lee,
And from the impurer matter free,
Becomes the richer still, the older,
And proves the pleasanter, the colder.

SAMUEL BUTLER

The Disappointment

One day the amorous Lysander,
By an impatient passion swayed,
Surprised fair Cloris, that loved maid,
Who could defend herself no longer.
All things did with his love conspire:
The gilded planet of the day
In his gay chariot drawn by fire
Was now descending to the sea,
And left no light to guide the world
But what from Cloris' brighter eyes was hurled.

In a lone thicket made for love,
Silent as yielding maid's consent,
She with a charming languishment
Permits his force, yet gently strove.
Her hands his bosom softly meet,
But not to put him back designed —
Rather to draw 'em on inclined.
Whilst he lay trembling at her feet
Resistance 'tis in vain to show:
She wants the power to say, 'Ah, what d'ye do?'

Her bright eyes sweet, and yet severe,
Where love and shame confusedly strive,
Fresh vigour to Lysander give;
And breathing faintly in his ear
She cried: 'Cease, cease your vain desire
Or I'll call out! What would you do?
My dearer honour even to you
I cannot, must not give! Retire!
Or take this life, whose chiefest part
I gave you with the conquest of my heart.'

But he as much unused to fear
As he was capable of love
The blessed minutes to improve
Kisses her mouth, her neck, her hair.
Each touch her new desire alarms,

258

His burning, trembling hand he pressed
Upon her swelling, snowy breast,
While she lay panting in his arms.
All her unguarded beauties lie
The spoils and trophies of the enemy.

And now without respect or fear
He seeks the object of his vows
(His love no modesty allows),
By swift degrees advancing — where
His daring hand that altar seized
Where gods of love do sacrifice:
That awful throne, that paradise
Where rage is calmed and anger pleased,
That fountain where delight still flows
And gives the universal world repose.

Her balmy lips encountering his,
Their bodies, as their souls, are joined
Where both in transports unconfined
Extend themselves upon the moss.
Cloris half dead and breathless lay,
Her soft eyes cast a humid light
Such as divides the day and night,
Or falling stars whose fires decay;
And now no signs of life she shows
But what in short-breathed sighs returns and goes.

He saw how at her length she lay.
He saw her rising bosom bare,
Her loose, thin robes, through which appear
A shape designed for love and play,
Abandoned by her pride and shame.
She does her softest joys dispense,
Offering her virgin-innocence
A victim to love's sacred flame,
While the o'er-ravished shepherd lies
Unable to perform the sacrifice.

Ready to taste a thousand joys
The too transported, hapless swain
Found the vast pleasure turned to pain —
Pleasure which too much love destroys.
The willing garments by he laid,
And heaven all opened to his view.
Mad to possess, himself he threw
On the defenceless, lovely maid.
But oh, what envying god conspires
To snatch his power, yet leave him the desire!

Nature's support (without whose aid
She can no human being give)
Itself now wants the art to live;
Faintness its slackened nerves invade.
In vain th'enraged youth essayed
To call its fleeting vigour back,
No motion 'twill from motion take.
Excess of love is Love betrayed.
In vain he toils, in vain commands —
Insensible falls weeping in his hands.

In this so amorous, cruel strife
Where love and fate were too severe
The poor Lysander in despair
Renounced his reason with his life.
Now all the brisk and active fire
That should the nobler part inflame
Served to increase his rage and shame
And left no spark for new desire.
Not all her naked charms could move
Or calm that rage that had debauched his love.

Cloris returning from the trance
Which love and soft desire had bred,
Her timorous hand she gently laid
(Or guided by desire or chance)
Upon that fabulous priapus,

That potent god, as poets feign —
But never did young shepherdess
Gathering of fern upon the plain
More nimbly draw her fingers back
Finding beneath the verdant leaves a snake

Than Cloris her fair hand withdrew,
Finding that god of her desires
Disarmed of all his awful fires
And cold as flowers bathed in the morning dew.
Who can the nymph's confusion guess?
The blood forsook the hinder place
And strewed with blushes all her face,
Which both disdain and shame expressed;
And from Lysander's arms she fled,
Leaving him fainting on the gloomy bed.

Like lightning through the groves she hies,
Or Daphne from the Delphic god;
No print upon the grassy road
She leaves, t'instruct pursuing eyes.
The wind that wantoned in her hair
And with her ruffled garments played
Discovered in the flying maid
All that the gods e'er made, if fair.
So Venus, when her love was slain,
With fear and haste flew o'er the fatal plain.

The nymph's resentments none but I
Can well imagine or condole.
But none can guess Lysander's soul
But those who swayed his destiny.
His silent griefs swell up to storms,
And not one god his fury spares;
He cursed his birth, his fate, his stars —
But more the shepherdess's charms,
Whose soft, bewitching influence
Had damned him to the hell of impotence.

MRS APHRA BENN

One Writing Against his Prick

Base metal hanger by your Master's Thigh!
Eternal shame to all Prick's heraldry,
Hide thy despised head and do not dare
To Peep, no not so much as take the air
But through a Button hole, but pine and die
Confin'd within the Codpiece Monastery.
The Little Childish Boy that hardly knows
The way through which his Urine flows
Toucht by my Mistress her Magnetic hand
His Little needle presently will stand.
Did she not raise thy drooping head on high
As it lay Nodding on her wanton thigh?
Did she not clap her legs about my back
Her Port hole open? Damn'd Prick what is't you
    lack?
Henceforth stand stiff and gain your credit lost
Or I'll ne'er draw thee, but against a Post.

ANON

Aubade

Hours before dawn we were woken by the quake.
My house was on a cliff. The thing could take
Bookloads off shelves, break bottles in a row.
Then the long pause and then the bigger shake.
It seemed the best thing to be up and go.

And far too large for my feet to step by.
I hoped that various buildings were brought low.
The heart of standing is you cannot fly.

It seemed quite safe till she got up and dressed.
The guarded tourist makes the guide the test.
Then I said The Garden? Laughing she said No.
Taxi for her and for me healthy rest.
It seemed the best thing to be up and go.

The language problem but you have to try.
Some solid ground for lying could she show?
The heart of standing is you cannot fly.

None of these deaths were her point at all.
The thing was that being woken he would bawl
And finding her not in earshot he would know.
I tried saying Half an Hour to pay this call.
It seemed the best thing to be up and go.

I slept, and blank as that I would yet lie.
Till you have seen what a threat holds below,
The heart of standing is you cannot fly.

Tell me again about Europe and her pains,
Who's tortured by the drought, who by the rains.
Glut me with floods where only the swine can row
Who cuts his throat and let him count his gains.
It seemed the best thing to be up and go.

263

A bedshift flight to a Far Eastern sky.
Only the same war on a stronger toe.
The heart of standing is you cannot fly.

Tell me more quickly what I lost by this,
Or tell me with less drama what they miss
Who call no die a god for a good throw,
Who say after two aliens had one kiss
It seemed the best thing to be up and go.

But as to risings, I can tell you why.
It is on contradiction that they grow.
It seemed the best thing to be up and go.
Up was the heartening and the strong reply.
The heart of standing is we cannot fly.

WILLIAM EMPSON

The Disabled Debauchee

As some brave admiral, in former war
 ·Deprived of force, but pressed with courage still,
Two rival fleets appearing from afar,
   Crawls to the top of an adjacent hill;

From whence, with thoughts full of concern, he views
   The wise and daring conduct of the fight,
Whilst each bold action to his mind renews
   His present glory and his past delight;

From his fierce eyes flashes of fire he throws,
   As from black clouds when lightning breaks away;
Transported, thinks himself amidst the foes,
   And absent, yet enjoys the bloody day;

So, when my days of impotence approach,
   And I'm by pox and wine's unlucky chance
Forced from the pleasing billows of debauch
   On the dull shore of lazy temperance,

My pains at least some respite shall afford
   While I behold the battles you maintain
When fleets of glasses sail about the board,
   From whose broadsides volleys of wit shall rain.

Nor let the sight of honourable scars,
   Which my too forward valour did procure,
Frighten new-listed soldiers from the wars:
   Past joys have more than paid what I endure.

Should any youth (worth being drunk) prove nice,
   And from his fair inviter meanly shrink,
'Twill please the ghost of my departed vice
   If, at my counsel, he repent and drink.

265

Or should some cold-complexioned sot forbid,
  With his dull morals, our bold night-alarms,
I'll fire his blood by telling what I did
  When I was strong and able to bear arms.

I'll tell of whores attacked, their lords at home;
  Bawds' quarters beaten up, and fortress won;
Windows demolished, watches overcome;
  And handsome ills by my contrivance done.

Nor shall our love-fits, Chloris, be forgot,
  When each the well-looked linkboy strove t' enjoy,
And the best kiss was the deciding lot
  Whether the boy fucked you, or I the boy.

With tales like these I will such thoughts inspire
  As to important mischief shall incline:
I'll make him long some ancient church to fire,
  And fear no lewdness he's called to by wine.

Thus, statesmanlike, I'll saucily impose,
  And safe from action, valiantly advise;
Sheltered in impotence, urge you to blows,
  And being good for nothing else, be wise.

JOHN WILMOT, EARL OF ROCHESTER

Song

By all love's soft, yet mighty powers,
   It is a thing unfit
That men should fuck in time of flowers,
   Or when the smock's beshit.

Fair nasty nymph, be clean and kind,
   And all my joys restore
By using paper still behind
   And spunges for before.

My spotless flames can ne'er decay
   If after every close,
My smoking prick escape the fray
   Without a bloody nose.

If thou wouldst have me true, be wise
   And take to cleanly sinning;
None but fresh lovers' pricks can rise
   At Phyllis in foul linen.

JOHN WILMOT, EARL OF ROCHESTER

A woman's face, with Nature's own hand painted

A woman's face, with Nature's own hand painted,
Hast thou, the master mistress of my passion;
A woman's gentle heart, but not acquainted
With shifting change, as is false women's fashion;
An eye more bright than theirs, less false in rolling.
Gilding the object whereupon it gazeth;
A man in hue all hues in his controlling,
Which steals men's eyes and women's souls amazeth.
And for a woman wert thou first created,
Till Nature as she wrought thee fell a-doting
And by addition me of thee defeated
By adding one thing to my purpose nothing.
   But since she prick'd thee out for women's pleasure,
   Mine be thy love, and thy love's use their treasure.

WILLIAM SHAKESPEARE

The Imperfect Enjoyment

Naked she lay, clasped in my longing arms,
I filled with love, and she all over charms;
Both equally inspired with eager fire,
Melting through kindness, flaming in desire.
With arms, legs, lips close clinging to embrace,
She clips me to her breast, and sucks me to her face.
Her nimble tongue, Love's lesser lightning, played
Within my mouth, and to my thoughts conveyed
Swift orders that I should prepare to throw
The all-dissolving thunderbolt below.
My fluttering soul, sprung with the pointed kiss,
Hangs hovering o'er her balmy brinks of bliss.
But whilst her busy hand would guide that part
Which should convey my soul up to her heart,
In liquid raptures I dissolve all o'er,
Melt into sperm, and spend at every pore.
A touch from any part of her had done 't:
Her hand, her foot, her very look's a cunt.
   Smiling, she chides in a kind murmuring noise,
And from her body wipes the clammy joys,
When, with a thousand kisses wandering o'er
My panting bosom, 'Is there then no more?'
She cries. 'All this to love and rapture's due;
Must we not pay a debt to pleasure too?'
   But I, the most forlorn, lost man alive,
To show my wished obedience vainly strive:
I sigh, alas! and kiss, but cannot swive.
Eager desires confound my first intent,
Succeeding shame does more success prevent,
And rage at last confirms me impotent.
Ev'n her fair hand, which might bid heat return
To frozen age, and make cold hermits burn,
Applied to my dead cinder, warms no more
Than fire to ashes could past flames restore.

swive: fuck

Trembling, confused, despairing, limber, dry,
A wishing, weak, unmoving lump I lie.
This dart of love, whose piercing point, oft tried,
With virgin blood ten thousand maids have dyed;
Which nature still directed with such art
That it through every cunt reached every heart —
Stiffly resolved, 'twould carelessly invade
Woman or man, nor ought its fury stayed:
Where'er it pierced, a cunt it found or made —
Now languid lies in this unhappy hour,
Shrunk up and sapless like a withered flower.
  Thou treacherous, base deserter of my flame,
False to my passion, fatal to my fame,
Through what mistaken magic dost thou prove
So true to lewdness, so untrue to love?
What oyster-cinder-beggar-common whore
Didst thou e'er fail in all thy life before?
When vice, disease, and scandal lead the way,
With what officious haste dost thou obey!
Like a rude, roaring hector in the streets
Who scuffles, cuffs, and justles all he meets,
But if his King or country claim his aid,
The rakehell villain shrinks and hides his head;
Ev'n so thy brutal valour is displayed,
Breaks every stew, does each small whore invade,
But when great Love the onset does command,
Base recreant to thy prince, thou dar'st not stand.
Worst part of me, and henceforth hated most,
Through all the town a common fucking post,
On whom each whore relieves her tingling cunt
As hogs on gates do rub themselves and grunt,
Mayst thou to ravenous chancres be a prey,
Or in consuming weepings waste away;

stew: brothel *weepings:* discharges

May strangury and stone thy days attend;
May'st thou ne'er piss, who didst refuse to spend
When all my joys did on false thee depend.
  And may ten thousand abler pricks agree
  To do the wronged Corinna right for thee.

JOHN WILMOT, EARL OF ROCHESTER

strangury: difficult urination

Fools

There is no fool like an old fool,
   Yet fools of middling age
Can seldom teach themselves to reach
   True folly's final stage.

Their course of love mounts not above
   Some five-and-forty years,
Though God gave men threescore and ten
   To scald with foolish tears.

ROBERT GRAVES

Acknowledgements

We should like to thank the following for permission to reproduce copyright material:

Kingsley Amis: from *A Look Round the Estate* published by Jonathan Cape, reprinted by permission of Random Century Group; Cliff Ashby: 'Cuckoo' and 'For Ann', reprinted by permission of the author; James Baxter: 'The Harlot' from *The Rock Woman: Selected Poems* (1969), reprinted by permission of Oxford University Press; Ronald Bottrall: 'Love in Umbria', reprinted by permission of Mrs Margot Bottrall; Robert Creeley: from *Poems 1950–1965*, reprinted by permission of Marion Boyars Publishers Ltd; e. e. cummings: from *Selected Poems 1923–1958* published by Mac-Gibbon & Kee, reprinted by permission of HarperCollins; Lawrence Durrell: from *Collected Poems 1935–1963*, reprinted by permission of Faber & Faber Ltd; William Empson: from *Collected Poems* published by The Hogarth Press, reprinted by permission of the Estate of William Empson and Random Century Group; Robert Graves: from *Collected Poems 1975*, reprinted by permission of A. P. Watt Limited on behalf of The Trustees of the Robert Graves Copyright Trust; Geoffrey Grigson: from *Sad Grave of an Imperial Mongoose* published by Macmillan, reprinted by permission of David Higham Associates Ltd; Erica Jong: from *Fruit and Vegetables* reprinted by permission of Martin Secker & Warburg; Robert Nye: 'Without Prejudice', reprinted by permission of the author; William Plomer: from *Collected Poems* published by Jonathan Cape, reprinted by permission of the Estate of William Plomer and Random Century Group; Ezra Pound: from *Selected Poems 1908–1959*, reprinted by permission of Faber & Faber Ltd; James Reeves: from *Collected Poems*, reprinted by permission of the Estate of

James Reeves and Anthony Beal; Anne Sexton: from *Love Poems* published by Oxford University Press, permission granted by Peters Fraser & Dunlop Ltd, and from *The Awful Rowing Towards God* published by Jonathan Cape, reprinted by permission of Random Century Group; C. H. Sisson: from *Collected Poems* published by Carcanet Press, reprinted by permission of the author; Bernard Spencer: 'Part of Plenty' © Mrs Anne Humphreys 1981, reprinted from Bernard Spencer's *Collected Poems* edited by Roger Bowen (1981) by permission of Oxford University Press; Arthur Symons: from *Arthur Symons: Selected Writings* edited by Roger Holdsworth, published by Carcanet Press.

Souvenir Press Ltd apologises for any errors or omissions in the above list and would be grateful for notification of any corrections which should be incorporated in any future reprint.

Index of Poets

Index of Titles

Index of Titles

Index of First Lines